D1209712

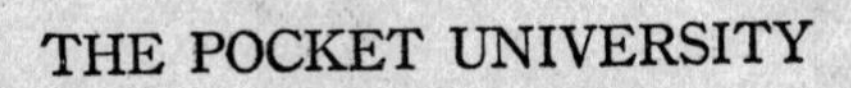
THE POCKET UNIVERSITY

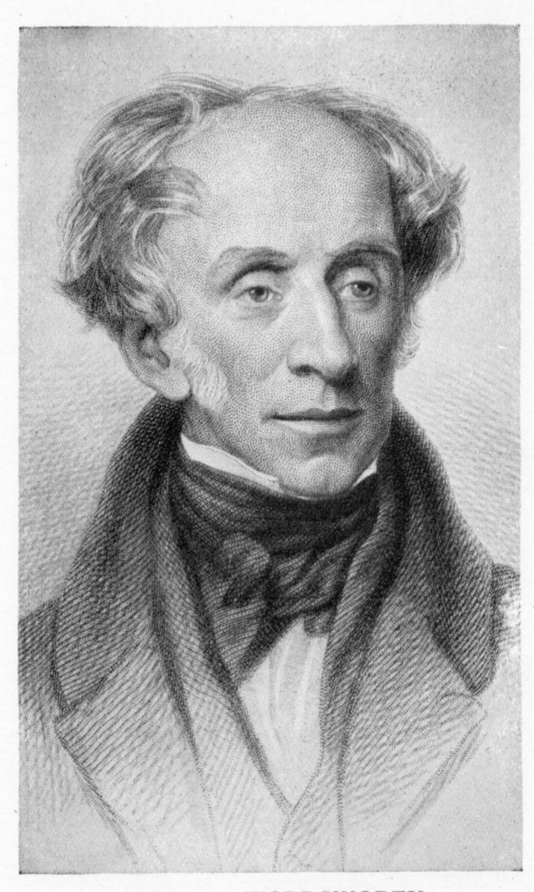

WILLIAM WORDSWORTH

THE POCKET UNIVERSITY

VOLUME XV

POETRY
ELEGIES AND HYMNS

EDITED BY
HENRY VAN DYKE

ASSISTED BY
HARDIN CRAIG, PH.D.
AND
ASA DON DICKINSON

PUBLISHED FOR
NELSON DOUBLEDAY, INC.
BY
DOUBLEDAY, PAGE & COMPANY
GARDEN CITY NEW YORK
1924

PRINTED IN THE UNITED STATES
AT
THE COUNTRY LIFE PRESS, GARDEN CITY, N. Y

CONTENTS

Contents

Contents

Contents

Selections from the Later Poetry

ELEGIES AND HYMNS

INTRODUCTION

THE poetry of love and mortal grief that has blossomed from the human heart under the shadow of death, and the poetry of trust and immortal hope that has unfolded in the light of religion,—these are flowers of the spirit whose pure and tender colours blend in a natural harmony. I have bound them together in this volume with the title *Elegies and Hymns.*

Elegy is a word which the Greeks and Romans used in a twofold sense: first, to describe any kind of mournful song or lament, even the wordless melody of the nightingale or the halcyon; and second, to denote a poem written in a certain metre, the so-called "elegiac verse" which consisted of alternate dactylic hexameters and pentameters, a smooth, restrained, pensive movement. In English poetry the latter sense is not often used, as the metre is one which it is difficult to imitate in our language, and there are but few examples of it. The former sense, in which the word is broadly applied to various forms of melancholy and regretful poetry, is familiar to critics. Coleridge attempted to make it broader still, defining elegy as "the form of poetry natural to the reflective mind." He asserts that "it may treat of any subject, but it must treat of no subject for itself, but always and exclusively with reference to the poet himself."

In the usage of the people, however, the word has taken a different course. It does not include the poetry of regret for fugitive pleasure or unrequited love, nor all the forms of verse in which the poet, to follow Coleridge's phrase, treats of his subject always and exclusively with reference to himself. These are classed with the pure lyrics, or with reflective verse. But an elegy, in common parlance, has come to mean a poem dealing with the thought or the fact of death. It is not an outward, metrical shape: it is an inward, spiritual form. It is the poetic utterance of the heart of man when he faces the sorrow of mortality. It is the voice in which he answers death and calls after the departed. It is the music with which he at once expresses and soothes the grief of the last farewell, pays tribute to vanished goodness and the memory of noble names, and encourages his own spirit to meet the end that comes to all, with fortitude and an equal mind.

It is in this sense that I have interpreted the sphere of elegiac poetry in this volume, bringing together the best of the shorter poems, of various types, in which the thought of death is central and controlling, and grouping them in six divisions, according to the different notes which they strike. First come the poems in which the subject of man's mortality is more broadly treated,

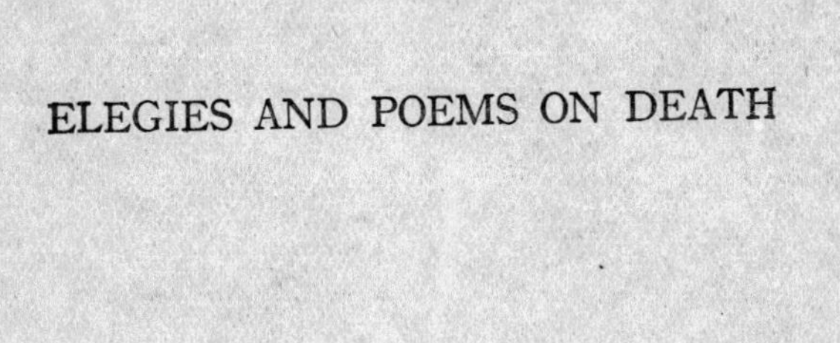

ELEGIES AND POEMS ON DEATH

DEATH THE LEVELLER

From *The Contention of Ajax and Ulysses.*

THE glories of our blood and state
  Are shadows, not substantial things;
There is no armour against Fate;
  Death lays his icy hand on kings:
      Sceptre and Crown
      Must tumble down,
And in the dust be equal made
With the poor crookèd scythe and spade.   8

Some men with swords may reap the field,
  And plant fresh laurels where they kill:
But their strong nerves at last must yield;
  They tame but one another still:
      Early or late
      They stoop to fate,
And must give up their murmuring breath,
When they, pale captives, creep to death.   16

The garlands wither on your brow,
  Then boast no more your mighty deeds;
Upon Death's purple altar now
  See where the victor-victim bleeds.
      Your heads must come
      To the cold tomb:
Only the actions of the just
Smell sweet and blossom in their dust.   24

1659.   *James Shirley.*

FRIENDS DEPARTED

THEY are all gone into the world of light!
And I alone sit ling'ring here;
Their very memory is fair and bright,
And my sad thoughts doth clear. 4

It glows and glitters in my cloudy breast,
Like stars upon some gloomy grove,
Or those faint beams in which this hill is drest
After the sun's remove. 8

I see them walking in an air of glory,
Whose light doth trample on my days:
My days, which are at best but dull and hoary,
Mere glimmering and decays. 12

O holy Hope! and high Humility,
High as the heavens above!
These are your walks, and you have show'd
them me,
To kindle my cold love. 16

Dear, beauteous Death! the jewel of the Just,
Shining nowhere, but in the dark;
What mysteries do lie beyond thy dust,
Could man outlook that mark! 20

Friends Departed

He that hath found some fledged bird's nest
　　　　may know,
　At first sight, if the bird be flown;
But what fair well or grove he sings in now,
　　　That is to him unknown. 24

And yet as Angels in some brighter dreams
　Call to the soul, when man doth sleep:
So some strange thoughts transcend our wonted
　　　　themes,
　　　And into glory peep. 28

If a star were confined into a tomb,
　Her captive flames must needs burn there;
But when the hand that lock'd her up gives
　　　　room,
　　　She'll shine through all the sphere. 32

O Father of eternal life, and all
　Created glories under Thee!
Resume Thy spirit from this world of thrall
　　　Into true liberty. 36

Either disperse these mists, which blot and fill
　My perspective still as they pass:
Or else remove me hence unto that hill,
　　　Where I shall need no glass. 40

1655. *Henry Vaughan.*

ELEGY WRITTEN IN A COUNTRY CHURCHYARD

THE curfew tolls the knell of parting day,
The lowing herd wind slowly o'er the lea,
The plowman homeward plods his weary way,
And leaves the world to darkness and to me. 4

Now fades the glimmering landscape on the sight,
And all the air a solemn stillness holds,
Save where the beetle wheels his droning flight,
And drowsy tinklings lull the distant folds; 8

Save that from yonder ivy-mantled tow'r
The moping owl does to the moon complain
Of such as, wand'ring near her secret bow'r,
Molest her ancient solitary reign. 12

Beneath those rugged elms, that yew-tree's shade,
Where heaves the turf in many a mould'ring heap,
Each in his narrow cell for ever laid,
The rude forefathers of the hamlet sleep. 16

The breezy call of incense-breathing morn,
  The swallow twitt'ring from the straw-built shed,
The cock's shrill clarion, or the echoing horn,
  No more shall rouse them from their lowly bed. 20

For them no more the blazing hearth shall burn,
  Or busy housewife ply her evening care;
No children run to lisp their sire's return,
  Or climb his knees the envied kiss to share. 24

Oft did the harvest to their sickle yield,
  Their furrow oft the stubborn glebe has broke;
How jocund did they drive their team afield!
  How bow'd the woods beneath their sturdy stroke! 28

Let not Ambition mock their useful toil,
  Their homely joys, and destiny obscure;
Nor Grandeur hear with a disdainful smile
  The short and simple annals of the poor. 32

The boast of heraldry, the pomp of pow'r,
  And all that beauty, all that wealth e'er gave,
Await alike th' inevitable hour:
  The paths of glory lead but to the grave. 36

Nor you, ye proud, impute to these the fault,
  If Memory o'er their tomb no trophies raise,

Where through the long-drawn aisle and fretted
vault
The pealing anthem swells the note of
praise. 40

Can storied urn or animated bust
Back to its mansion call the fleeting breath?
Can Honour's voice provoke the silent dust,
Or Flatt'ry soothe the dull cold ear of
Death? 44

Perhaps in this neglected spot is laid
Some heart once pregnant with celestial fire;
Hands, that the rod of empire might have
sway'd,
Or waked to ecstasy the living lyre. 48

But Knowledge to their eyes her ample page
Rich with the spoils of time did ne'er unroll;
Chill Penury repress'd their noble rage,
And froze the genial current of the soul. 52

Full many a gem of purest ray serene
The dark unfathom'd caves of ocean bear;
Full many a flower is born to blush unseen,
And waste its sweetness on the desert air. 56

Some village Hampden that with dauntless
breast
The little tyrant of his fields withstood;
Some mute inglorious Milton here may rest,
Some Cromwell guiltless of his country's
blood. 60

Th' applause of list'ning senates to command,
The threats of pain and ruin to despise,
To scatter plenty o'er a smiling land,
And read their history in a nation's eyes,— 64

Their lot forbade: nor circumscribed alone
Their growing virtues, but their crimes confined;
Forbade to wade thro' slaughter to a throne,
And shut the gates of mercy on mankind. 68

The struggling pangs of conscious truth to hide,
To quench the blushes of ingenuous shame,
Or heap the shrine of Luxury and Pride
With incense kindled at the Muse's flame. 72

Far from the madding crowd's ignoble strife
Their sober wishes never learn'd to stray;
Along the cool, sequester'd vale of life
They kept the noiseless tenor of their way. 76

Yet ev'n these bones from insult to protect
Some frail memorial still erected nigh,
With uncouth rhymes and shapeless sculpture deck'd,
Implores the passing tribute of a sigh. 80

Their name, their years, spelt by th' unletter'd Muse,
The place of fame and elegy supply;
And many a holy text around she strews,
That teach the rustic moralist to die. 84

For who, to dumb Forgetfulness a prey,
  This pleasing anxious being e'er resign'd,
Left the warm precincts of the cheerful day,
  Nor cast one longing ling'ring look behind? 88

On some fond breast the parting soul relies,
  Some pious drops the closing eye requires;
E'en from the tomb the voice of Nature cries,
  E'en in our ashes live their wonted fires. 92

For thee, who, mindful of th' unhonour'd dead,
  Dost in these lines their artless tale relate;
If chance, by lonely contemplation led,
  Some kindred spirit shall inquire thy fate,—96

Haply some hoary-headed swain may say,
"Oft have we seen him at the peep of dawn
Brushing with hasty steps the dews away
  To meet the sun upon the upland lawn. 100

"There at the foot of yonder nodding beech
  That wreathes its old fantastic roots so high,
His listless length at noontide would he stretch,
  And pore upon the brook that babbles by. 104

"Hard by yon wood, now smiling as in scorn,
  Mutt'ring his wayward fancies he would rove,
Now drooping, woeful-wan, like one forlorn,
  Or crazed with care, or cross'd in hopeless
    love. 108

"One morn I miss'd him on the custom'd hill,
Along the heath, and near his favourite tree;
Another came; nor yet beside the rill,
Nor up the lawn, nor at the wood was he: 112

"The next with dirges due in sad array
Slow through the church-way path we saw him borne.
Approach and read (for thou canst read) the lay
Graved on the stone beneath yon agèd thorn:" 116

THE EPITAPH

Here rests his head upon the lap of Earth
A Youth, to Fortune and to Fame unknown.
Fair Science frown'd not on his humble birth,
And Melancholy mark'd him for her own. 120

Large was his bounty, and his soul sincere,
Heav'n did a recompense as largely send;
He gave to Mis'ry all he had, a tear,
He gain'd from Heav'n ('t was all he wish'd) a friend. 124

No farther seek his merits to disclose,
Or draw his frailties from their dread abode,
(There they alike in trembling hope repose,)
The bosom of his Father and his God. 128

1751. *Thomas Gray.*

THANATOPSIS

To him who, in the love of Nature, holds
Communion with her visible forms, she speaks
A various language: for his gayer hours
She has a voice of gladness, and a smile
And eloquence of beauty; and she glides
Into his darker musings with a mild
And healing sympathy, that steals away
Their sharpness, ere he is aware. When thoughts
Of the last bitter hour come like a blight
Over thy spirit, and sad images 10
Of the stern agony, and shroud, and pall,
And breathless darkness, and the narrow house,
Make thee to shudder, and grow sick at heart—
Go forth under the open sky, and list
To Nature's teachings, while from all around—
Earth and her waters, and the depths of air—
Comes a still voice:—Yet a few days, and thee
The all-beholding sun shall see no more
In all his course; nor yet in the cold ground,
Where thy pale form was laid, with many tears, 20
Nor in the embrace of ocean, shall exist
Thy image. Earth, that nourished thee, shall
    claim
Thy growth, to be resolved to earth again;
And, lost each human trace, surrendering up

Thine individual being, shalt thou go
To mix forever with the elements,
To be a brother to the insensible rock,
And to the sluggish clod, which the rude swain
Turns with his share, and treads upon. The oak
Shall send his roots abroad, and pierce thy
mould. 30

Yet not to thine eternal resting-place
Shalt thou retire alone,—nor couldst thou wish
Couch more magnificent. Thou shalt lie down
With patriarchs of the infant world,—with kings,
The powerful of the earth,—the wise, the good,
Fair forms, and hoary seers of ages past,
All in one mighty sepulchre. The hills,
Rock-ribbed, and ancient as the sun; the vales
Stretching in pensive quietness between;
The venerable woods; rivers that move 40
In majesty, and the complaining brooks,
That make the meadows green; and, poured
round all,
Old ocean's gray and melancholy waste,—
Are but the solemn decorations all
Of the great tomb of man! The golden sun,
The planets, all the infinite host of heaven,
Are shining on the sad abodes of death,
Through the still lapse of ages. All that tread
The globe are but a handful to the tribes
That slumber in its bosom. Take the wings 50
Of morning, pierce the Barcan wilderness,
Or lose thyself in the continuous woods
Where rolls the Oregon, and hears no sound
Save his own dashings,—yet the dead are there!

And millions in those solitudes, since first
The flight of years began, have laid them down
In their last sleep,—the dead reign there alone!
So shalt thou rest; and what if thou withdraw
In silence from the living, and no friend
Take note of thy departure? All that breathe 60
Will share thy destiny. The gay will laugh
When thou art gone, the solemn brood of care
Plod on, and each one, as before, will chase
His favorite phantom; yet all these shall leave
Their mirth and their employments, and shall
come
And make their bed with thee. As the long train
Of ages glide away, the sons of men—
The youth in life's green spring, and he who goes
In the full strength of years, matron and maid,
And the sweet babe, and the gray-headed man— 70
Shall, one by one, be gathered to thy side
By those who in their turn shall follow them.

So live, that when thy summons comes to join
The innumerable caravan that moves
To the pale realms of shade, where each shall
take
His chamber in the silent halls of death,
Thou go not, like the quarry-slave at night,
Scourged to his dungeon, but, sustained and
soothed
By an unfaltering trust, approach thy grave
Like one who wraps the drapery of his couch 80
About him, and lies down to pleasant dreams.

1817. *William Cullen Bryant.*

SLEEP

"He giveth his beloved sleep."—*Psalm* cxxvi, 2.

Of all the thoughts of God that are
Borne inward unto souls afar,
Along the Psalmist's music deep,
Now tell me if that any is,
For gift or grace, surpassing this,—
"He giveth his belovèd—sleep"? 6

What would we give to our beloved?
The hero's heart, to be unmoved,—
The poet's star-tuned harp, to sweep,—
The patriot's voice, to teach and rouse,—
The monarch's crown, to light the brows?
"He giveth *his* belovèd—sleep." 12

What do we give to our beloved?
A little faith, all undisproved,—
A little dust to overweep,
And bitter memories, to make
The whole earth blasted for our sake,
"He giveth *his* belovèd—sleep." 18

"Sleep soft, beloved!" we sometimes say,
But have no tune to charm away

Sad dreams that through the eyelids creep;
But never doleful dream again
Shall break the happy slumber when
"He giveth *his* belovèd—sleep." 24

O earth, so full of dreary noises!
O men, with wailing in your voices!
O delvèd gold the wailers heap!
O strife, O curse, that o'er it fall!
God strikes a silence through you all,
And "giveth his belovèd—sleep." 30

Ay, men may wonder while they scan
A living, thinking, feeling man
Confirmed in such a rest to keep;
But angels say, and through the word
I think their happy smile is *heard*—
"He giveth his belovèd—sleep." 36

His dews drop mutely on the hill,
His cloud above it saileth still,
Though on its slope men sow and reap;
More softly than the dew is shed,
Or cloud is floated overhead,
"He giveth his belovèd—sleep." 42

For me, my heart, that erst did go
Most like a tired child at a show,
That sees through tears the mummers leap,
Would now its wearied vision close,
Would childlike on his love repose
Who "giveth his belovèd—sleep." 48

And friends, dear friends, when it shall be
That his low breath is gone from me,
And round my bier ye come to weep,
Let one, most loving of you all,
Say "Not a tear must o'er her fall!
He giveth his belovèd sleep." 54

1838. *Elizabeth Barrett Browning.*

THE DESERTED HOUSE

LIFE and Thought have gone away
Side by side,
Leaving door and windows wide:
Careless tenants they! 4

All within is dark as night;
In the windows is no light;
And no murmur at the door,
So frequent on its hinge before. 8

Close the door, the shutters close,
Or thro' the windows we shall see
The nakedness and vacancy
Of the dark, deserted house. 12

Come away: no more of mirth
Is here or merry-making sound.
The house was builded of the earth,
And shall fall again to ground. 16

Come away: for Life and Thought
  Here no longer dwell;
    But in a city glorious—
A great and distant city—have bought
  A mansion incorruptible.
Would they could have staid with us! 22

1830. *Lord Tennyson.*

PROEM TO—*IN MEMORIAM*

Strong Son of God, immortal Love,
  Whom we, that have not seen thy face,
  By faith, and faith alone, embrace,
Believing where we cannot prove; 4

Thine are these orbs of light and shade;
  Thou madest Life in man and brute;
  Thou madest Death; and lo, thy foot
Is on the skull which thou hast made. 8

Thou wilt not leave us in the dust:
  Thou madest man, he knows not why,
  He thinks he was not made to die;
And thou hast made him: thou art just. 12

Thou seemest human and divine,
  The highest, holiest manhood, thou:
  Our wills are ours, we know not how;
Our wills are ours, to make them thine. 16

Our little systems have their day,
They have their day and cease to be:
They are but broken lights of thee,
And thou, O Lord, art more than they. 20

We have but faith: we cannot know;
For knowledge is of things we see;
And yet we trust it comes from thee,
A beam in darkness: let it grow. 24

Let knowledge grow from more to more,
But more of reverence in us dwell;
That mind and soul, according well,
May make one music as before, 28

But vaster. We are fools and slight;
We mock thee when we do not fear:
But help thy foolish ones to bear;
Help thy vain worlds to bear thy light. 32

Forgive what seem'd my sin in me;
What seem'd my worth since I began;
For merit lives from man to man,
And not from man, O Lord, to thee. 36

Forgive my grief for one removed,
Thy creature, whom I found so fair.
I trust he lives in thee, and there
I find him worthier to be loved. 40

Forgive these wild and wandering cries,
Confusions of a wasted youth;
Forgive them where they fail in truth,
And in thy wisdom make me wise. 44

1849. *Lord Tennyson.*

THE BATTLE-FIELD

Once this soft turf, this rivulet's sands,
Were trampled by a hurrying crowd,
And fiery hearts and armèd hands
Encountered in the battle-cloud. 4

Ah! never shall the land forget
How gushed the life-blood of her brave,—
Gushed, warm with hope and courage yet,
Upon the soil they fought to save. 8

Now all is calm and fresh and still;
Alone the chirp of flitting bird,
And talk of children on the hill,
And bell of wandering kine, are heard. 12

No solemn host goes trailing by
The black-mouthed gun and staggering wain;
Men start not at the battle-cry,—
Oh, be it never heard again! 16

THE TOMB OF GRAY
In the churchyard of Stoke Poges, near Windsor

Soon rested those who fought; but thou
  Who minglest in the harder strife
For truths which men receive not now,
  Thy warfare only ends with life. 20

A friendless warfare! lingering long
  Through weary day and weary year;
A wild and many-weaponed throng
  Hang on thy front and flank and rear. 24

Yet nerve thy spirit to the proof,
  And blench not at thy chosen lot;
The timid good may stand aloof,
  The sage may frown,—yet faint thou not. 28

Nor heed the shaft too surely cast,
  The foul and hissing bolt of scorn;
For with thy side shall dwell, at last,
  The victory of endurance born. 32

Truth, crushed to earth, shall rise again,—
  Th' eternal years of God are hers;
But Error, wounded, writhes in pain,
  And dies among his worshippers. 36

Yea, though thou lie upon the dust,
  When they who helped thee flee in fear,
Die full of hope and manly trust,
  Like those who fell in battle here! 40

Another hand thy sword shall wield,
  Another hand the standard wave,
Till from the trumpet's mouth is pealed
  The blast of triumph o'er thy grave. 44

1837. *William Cullen Bryant.*

THE BIVOUAC OF THE DEAD

The muffled drum's sad roll has beat
  The soldier's last tattoo;
No more on Life's parade shall meet
  That brave and fallen few.
On Fame's eternal camping-ground
  Their silent tents are spread,
And Glory guards, with solemn round,
  The bivouac of the dead. 8

No rumor of the foe's advance
  Now swells upon the wind;
No troubled thought at midnight haunts
  Of loved ones left behind;
No vision of the morrow's strife
  The warrior's dream alarms;
No braying horn nor screaming fife
  At dawn shall call to arms. 16

Their shivered swords are red with rust,
  Their plumèd heads are bowed;
Their haughty banner, trailed in dust,
  Is now now their martial shroud.

And plenteous funeral tears have washed
  The red stains from each brow,
And the proud forms, by battle gashed,
  Are free from Anguish now. 24

The neighing troop, the flashing blade,
  The bugle's stirring blast,
The charge, the dreadful cannonade,
  The din and shout, are past;
Nor war's wild note nor glory's peal
  Shall thrill with fierce delight
Those breasts that never more may feel
  The rapture of the fight. 32

Like the fierce northern hurricane
  That sweeps his great plateau,
Flushed with the triumph yet to gain,
  Came down the serried foe.
Who heard the thunder of the fray
  Break o'er the field beneath,
Knew well the watchword of that day
  Was "Victory or Death." 40

Long had the doubtful conflict raged
  O'er all that stricken plain,
For never fiercer fight had waged
  The vengeful blood of Spain;
And still the storm of battle blew,
  Still swelled the gory tide;
Not long, our stout old chieftain knew,
  Such odds his strength could bide. 48

'T was in that hour his stern command
  Called to a martyr's grave
The flower of his belovèd land,
  The nation's flag to save.
By rivers of their fathers' gore
  His first-born laurels grew,
And well he deemed the sons would pour
  Their lives for glory too. 56

Full many a norther's breath has swept
  O'er Angostura's plain,
And long the pitying sky has wept
  Above its mouldered slain.
The raven's scream, or eagle's flight,
  Or shepherd's pensive lay,
Alone awakes each sullen height
  That frowned o'er that dread fray. 64

Sons of the Dark and Bloody Ground,
  Ye must not slumber there,
Where stranger steps and tongues resound
  Along the heedless air.
Your own proud land's heroic soil
  Shall be your fitter grave:
She claims from war his richest spoil—
  The ashes of her brave. 72

Thus 'neath their parent turf they rest,
  Far from the gory field,
Borne to a Spartan mother's breast
  On many a bloody shield;

The sunshine of their native sky
  Smiles sadly on them here,
And kindred eyes and hearts watch by
  The heroes' sepulchre. 80

Rest on, embalmed and sainted dead!
  Dear as the blood ye gave;
No impious footstep here shall tread
  The herbage of your grave;
Nor shall your glory be forgot
  While Fame her record keeps,
Or Honor points the hallowed spot
  Where Valor proudly sleeps. 88

Yon marble minstrel's voiceless stone
  In deathless song shall tell,
When many a vanished age hath flown,
  The story how ye fell;
Nor wreck, nor change, nor winter's blight,
  Nor Time's remorseless doom,
Shall dim one ray of glory's light
  That gilds your deathless tomb. 96

1847. *Theodore O'Hara.*

THE BURIAL OF SIR JOHN MOORE AFTER CORUNNA

Not a drum was heard, not a funeral note,
  As his corse to the rampart we hurried;
Not a soldier discharged his farewell shot
  O'er the grave where our hero we buried. 4

We buried him darkly at dead of night,
  The sods with our bayonets turning,
By the struggling moonbeam's misty light
  And the lanthorn dimly burning. 8

No useless coffin enclosed his breast,
  Not in sheet or in shroud we wound him;
But he lay like a warrior taking his rest
  With his martial cloak around him. 12

Few and short were the prayers we said,
  And we spoke not a word of sorrow;
But we steadfastly gazed on the face that was
    dead,
  And we bitterly thought of the morrow. 16

We thought as we hollow'd his narrow bed,
  And smooth'd down his lonely pillow,
That the foe and the stranger would tread o'er
    his head,
  And we far away on the billow! 20

Lightly they 'll talk of the spirit that 's gone,
  And o'er his cold ashes upbraid him,—
But little he 'll reck, if they let him sleep on
  In the grave where a Briton has laid him. 24

But half of our heavy task was done
  When the clock struck the hour for retiring;
And we heard the distant and random gun
  That the foe was sullenly firing. 28

Slowly and sadly we laid him down,
  From the field of his fame fresh and gory;
We carved not a line, and we raised not a stone,
  But we left him alone with his glory. 32

1817. *Charles Wolfe.*

CORONACH

From *The Lady of the Lake*

He is gone on the mountain,
  He is lost to the forest,
Like a summer-dried fountain,
  When our need was the sorest.
The fount, reappearing,
  From the raindrops shall borrow,
But to us comes no cheering,
  To Duncan no morrow! 8

The hand of the reaper
  Takes the ears that are hoary,
But the voice of the weeper
  Wails manhood in glory.
The autumn winds rushing
  Waft the leaves that are serest,
But our flower was in flushing,
  When blighting was nearest. 16

Fleet foot on the correi,
  Sage counsel in cumber,
Red hand in the foray,
  How sound is thy slumber!

Like the dew on the mountain,
Like the foam on the river,
Like the bubble on the fountain,
Thou art gone; and for ever! 24

1810. *Sir Walter Scott.*

ODE WRITTEN IN 1745

How sleep the brave who sink to rest,
By all their country's wishes blest!
When Spring, with dewy fingers cold,
Returns to deck their hallow'd mould,
She there shall dress a sweeter sod
Than Fancy's feet have ever trod. 6

By fairy hands their knell is rung;
By forms unseen their dirge is sung;
There Honour comes, a pilgrim grey,
To bless the turf that wraps their clay;
And Freedom shall awhile repair,
To dwell, a weeping hermit, there! 12

1746. *William Collins.*

MAGNOLIA CEMETERY

Sung at Charleston, S. C., over the graves of the Confederate Soldiers

Sleep sweetly in your humble graves,
Sleep, martyrs of a fallen cause!
Though yet no marble column craves
The pilgrim here to pause. 4

In seeds of laurel in the earth
  The blossom of your fame is blown,
And somewhere, waiting for its birth,
  The shaft is in the stone! 8

Meanwhile, behalf the tardy years
  Which keep in trust your storied tombs,
Behold! your sisters bring their tears,
  And these memorial blooms. 12

Small tributes! but your shades will smile
  More proudly on these wreaths to-day,
Than when some cannon-moulded pile
  Shall overlook this bay. 16

Stoop, angels, hither from the skies!
  There is no holier spot of ground
Than where defeated valor lies,
  By mourning beauty crowned! 20

1867. *Henry Timrod.*

A LYKE-WAKE DIRGE

THIS ae nighte, this ae nighte,
—Every nighte and alle,
Fire and sleet and candle-lighte,
  And Christe receive thy saule. 4

When thou from hence away art past,
—Every nighte and alle,
To Whinny-muir thou com'st at last;
  And Christe receive thy saule. 8

If ever thou gavest hosen and shoon,
—Every nighte and alle,
Sit thee down and put them on;
  And Christe receive thy saule. 12

If hosen and shoon thou ne'er gav'st nane,
—Every nighte and alle,
The whinnes sall prick thee to the bare bane;
  And Christe receive thy saule. 16

From Whinny-muir when thou may'st pass,
—Every nighte and alle,
To Brig o' Dread thou com'st at last;
  And Christe receive thy saule. 20

From Brig o' Dread when thou may'st pass,
—Every nighte and alle,
To Purgatory fire thou com'st at last;
  And Christe receive thy saule. 24

If ever thou gavest meat or drink,
—Every nighte and alle,
The fire sall never make thee shrink;
  And Christe receive thy saule. 28

If meat or drink thou ne'er gav'st nane,
—Every nighte and alle,
The fire will burn thee to the bare bane;
  And Christe receive thy saule. 32

This ae nighte, this ae nighte,
—Every nighte and alle,
Fire and sleet and candle-lighte,
  And Christe receive thy saule. 36

Scott, Minst. Scot. Bord.

"FEAR NO MORE THE HEAT O' THE SUN"

From *Cymbeline*

FEAR no more the heat o' the sun,
  Nor the furious winter's rages;
Thou thy worldly task hast done,
  Home art gone, and ta'en thy wages:
Golden lads and girls all must,
As chimney-sweepers, come to dust. 6

Fear no more the frown o' the great,
  Thou are past the tyrant's stroke;
Care no more to clothe, and eat;
  To thee the reed is as the oak:
The sceptre, learning, physic, must
All follow this, and come to dust. 12

Fear no more the lightning-flash
  Nor the all-dreaded thunder-stone;
Fear not slander, censure rash;
  Thou hast finished joy and moan:
All lovers young, all lovers must
Consign to thee, and come to dust. 18

1623. *William Shakespeare.*

A SEA DIRGE

From *The Tempest*

FULL fathom five thy father lies:
Of his bones are coral made;
Those are pearls that were his eyes:
Nothing of him that doth fade
But doth suffer a sea-change
Into something rich and strange.
Sea-nymphs hourly ring his knell:
Hark! now I hear them,—Ding-dong,
bell!

1623. *William Shakespeare.*

THE SHROUDING OF THE DUCHESS OF MALFI

From *The Duchess of Malfi*

HARK! Now everything is still,
The screech-owl and the whistler shrill,
Call upon our dame aloud,
And bid her quickly don her shroud! 4

A Dirge

Much you had of land and rent;
Your length in clay 's now competent:
A long war disturb'd your mind;
Here your perfect peace is sign'd. 8

Of what is 't fools make such vain keeping?
Sin their conception, their birth weeping,
Their life a general mist of error,
Their death a hideous storm of terror.
Strew your hair with powders sweet,
Don clean linen, bathe your feet, 14

And—the foul end more to check—
A crucifix let bless your neck:
'T is now full tide 'tween night and day;
End your groan and come away. 18

1612? 1623. *John Webster*

A DIRGE

From *The White Devil.*

Call for the robin-redbreast and the wren,
Since o'er the shady groves they hover,
And with leaves and flowers do cover
The friendless bodies of unburied men.
Call unto his funeral dole
The ant, the field-mouse, and the mole,

To rear him hillocks that shall keep him warm,
And (when gay tombs are robb'd) sustain no
 harm;
But keep the wolf far thence, that 's foe to men,
For with his nails he 'll dig them up again. 10

1612. *John Webster.*

MINSTREL'S SONG

From *Ælla*

OH sing unto my roundelay!
 Oh drop the briny tear with me!
Dance no more at holiday;
 Like a running river be.
 My love is dead,
 Gone to his death-bed,
 All under the willow-tree. 7

Black his hair as the winter night,
 White his skin as the summer snow,
Ruddy his face as the morning light;
 Cold he lies in the grave below. 11

Sweet his tongue as the throstle's note;
 Quick in dance as thought can be;
Deft his tabor, cudgel stout;
 Oh! he lies by the willow-tree! 15

Hark! the raven flaps his wing
 In the briered dell below;
Hark! the death-owl loud doth sing
 To the nightmares as they go. 19

Lacrimæ

See! the white moon shines on high;
  Whiter is my true-love's shroud,
Whiter than the morning sky,
  Whiter than the evening cloud. 23

Here, upon my true-love's grave
  Shall the barren flowers be laid,
Not one holy saint to save
  All the coldness of a maid. 27

With my hands I 'll fix the briers
  Round his holy corse to gre;
Elfin fairies, light your fires;
  Here my body still shall be. 31

Come, with acorn-cup and thorn,
  Drain my heart's blood away;
Life and all its good I scorn,
  Dance by night, or feast by day. 35

Water-witches, crowned with reytes,
  Bear me to your lethal tide.
I die! I come! my true-love waits.
  Thus the damsel spake, and died. 39

1769. 1777. *Thomas Chatterton.*

LACRIMÆ

CALL me no more,
As heretofore,
The music of a feast;
Since now, alas!
The mirth that was
In me, is dead or ceas'd. 6

Before I went
To banishment
Into the loathèd west,
I could rehearse
A lyric verse,
And speak it with the best. 12

But time, ah me!
Has laid, I see,
My organ fast asleep;
And turn'd my voice
Into the noise
Of those that sit and weep. 18

1648. *Robert Herrick.*

WOLFRAM'S DIRGE

From *Death's Jest-Book*

If thou wilt ease thine heart
Of love and all its smart,
Then sleep, dear, sleep!
And not a sorrow
Hang any tear on your eyelashes;
Lie still and deep,
Sad soul, until the sea-wave washes
The rim o' the sun to-morrow,
In eastern sky. 9

But wilt thou cure thine heart
Of love and all its smart,
Then die, dear, die!

The Last Word

'T is deeper, sweeter,
Than on a rose bank to lie dreaming
With folded eye;
And then alone, amid the beaming
Of love's stars, thou 'lt meet her
In eastern sky. 18

1850. *Thomas Lovell Beddoes.*

THE LAST WORD

Creep into thy narrow bed,
Creep, and let no more be said!
Vain thy onset! all stands fast.
Thou thyself must break at last. 4

Let the long contention cease!
Geese are swans, and swans are geese.
Let them have it how they will!
Thou art tired; best be still. 8

They out-talk'd thee, hiss'd thee, tore thee?
Better men fared thus before thee;
Fired their ringing shot and pass'd,
Hotly charged—and sank at last. 12

Charge once more, then, and be dumb!
Let the victors, when they come,
When the forts of folly fall,
Find thy body by the wall! 16

1867. *Matthew Arnold.*

AN EPITAPH ON THE ADMIRABLE DRAMATIC POET, W. SHAKESPEARE

What needs my Shakespeare for his honoured
bones,
The labour of an age in pilèd stones?
Or that his hallowed relics should be hid
Under a star-y-pointing pyramid?
Dear son of memory, great heir of fame,
What need'st thou such weak witness of thy
name?
Thou in our wonder and astonishment
Hast built thyself a livelong monument.
For whilst, to the shame of slow-endeavouring
art,
Thy easy numbers flow, and that each heart 10
Hath from the leaves of thy unvalued book
Those Delphic lines with deep impression took;
Then thou our fancy of itself bereaving,
Dost make us marble with too much conceiving;
And so sepulchred in such pomp dost lie,
That kings for such a tomb would wish to die.

1632. *John Milton.*

ELEGY ON SHAKESPEARE

RENOWNÈD Spenser lie a thought more nigh
To learnèd Chaucer, and rare Beaumont lie
A little nearer Spenser, to make room
For Shakespeare in your threefold, fourfold
tomb.
To lodge all four in one bed make a shift
Until Doomsday, for hardly will a fift
Betwixt this day and that by Fate be slain,
For whom your curtains may be drawn again.
If your precedency in death doth bar
A fourth place in your sacred sepulchre, 10
Under this carved marble of thine own,
Sleep, rare Tragedian, Shakespeare, sleep alone:
Thy unmolested peace, unshared cave
Possess as lord, not tenant, of thy grave,
That unto us and others it may be
Honour hereafter to be laid by thee.

1633. *William Basse.*

ON THE TOMBS IN WESTMINSTER

MORTALITY, behold and fear!
What a change of flesh is here!
Think how many royal bones
Sleep within these heaps of stones;

Here they lie had realms and lands,
Who now want strength to stir their hands,
Where from their pulpits seal'd with dust
They preach, "In greatness is no trust."
Here 's an acre sown indeed
With the richest, royallest seed 10
That the earth did e'er suck in
Since the first man died for sin:
Here the bones of birth have cried
"Though gods they were, as men they died!"
Here are sands, ignoble things,
Dropt from the ruin'd sides of kings:
Here 's a world of pomp and state
Buried in dust, once dead by fate.

1653. *Francis Beaumont.*

EPITAPH ON THE COUNTESS OF PEMBROKE

UNDERNEATH this sable hearse
Lies the subject of all verse,
Sydney's sister, Pembroke's mother;
Death, ere thou hast slain another
Learn'd and fair, and good as she,
Time shall throw a dart at thee. 6

Marble piles let no man raise
To her name, for after days;

Some kind woman, born as she,
Reading this, like Niobe,
Shall turn statue, and become
Both her mourner and her tomb. 12

1641. *Ben. Jonson.*

ON ELIZABETH L. H.

Wouldst thou hear what Man can say
In a little? Reader, stay.
Underneath this stone doth lie
As much Beauty as could die:
Which in life did harbour give
To more Virtue than doth live.
If at all she had a fault,
Leave it buried in this vault.
One name was *Elizabeth,*
The other, let it sleep with death: 10
Fitter, where it died, to tell,
Than that it lived at all. Farewell!

1616. *Ben. Jonson.*

UPON THE DEATH OF SIR ALBERT MORTON'S WIFE

He first deceased; she for a little tried
To live without him, liked it not, and died.

1627. *Sir Henry Wotton.*

EPITAPH

On the Lady Mary Villiers

The Lady Mary Villiers lies
Under this stone; with weeping eyes
The parents that first gave her birth,
And their sad friends, laid her in earth.
If any of them, Reader, were
Known unto thee, shed a tear;
Or if thyself possess a gem,
As dear to thee, as this to them;
Though a stranger to this place,
Bewail in theirs thine own hard case: 10
For thou perhaps at thy return
May'st find thy Darling in an urn.

1640. *Thomas Carew.*

A NAMELESS EPITAPH

Ask not my name, O friend!
That Being only, which hath known each man
From the beginning, can
Remember each unto the end.

1867. *Matthew Arnold.*

V

ON SIR PHILIP SIDNEY

SILENCE augmenteth grief, writing increaseth rage,
Stal'd are my thoughts, which loved and lost, the wonder of our age,
Yet quickened now with fire, though dead with frost ere now,
Enraged I write I know not what: dead quick, I know not how. 4

Hard-hearted minds relent, and Rigor's tears abound,
And Envy strangely rues his end, in whom no fault she found;
Knowledge his light hath lost, Valor hath slain her knight:
Sidney is dead, dead is my friend, dead is the world's delight. 8

Place pensive wailes his fall, whose presence was her pride,
Time crieth out, my ebb is come, his life was my spring-tide;

Fame mourns in that she lost, the ground of her
reports,
Each living wight laments his lack, and all in
sundry sorts. 12

He was—woe worth that word—to each well
thinking mind,
A spotless friend, a matchless man, whose
virtue ever shined,
Declaring in his thoughts, his life, and that he
writ,
Highest conceits, longest foresights, and deepest
works of wit. 16

He only like himself, was second unto none,
Where death—though life—we rue, and wrong,
and all in vain do moan,
Their loss, not him wail they, that fill the world
with cries,
Death slew not him, but he made death his
ladder to the skies. 20

Now sink of sorrow I, who live, the more the
wrong,
Who wishing Death, whom death denies, whose
thread is all too long,
Who tied to wretched life, who look for no relief,
Must spend my ever-dying days in never-ending
grief. 24

Heart's ease and only I, like parallels run on,
Whose equal length, keep equal breadth, and
never meet in one,

Yet for not wronging him, my thoughts, my
sorrows' cell,
Shall not run out, though leak they will, for
liking him so well. 28

Farewell to you my hopes, my wonted waking
dreams,
Farewell sometime enjoyed joy eclipsed are
thy beams,
Farewell self-pleasing thoughts, which quietness
brings forth,
And farewell friendship's sacred league uniting
minds of worth. 32

And farewell merry heart, the gift of guiltless
minds,
And all sports, which for live's restore, variety
assigns,
Let all that sweet is, void? in me no mirth may
dwell,
Philip the cause of all this woe, my life 's content,
farewell. 36

Now rime, the source of rage, which art no kin
to skill,
And endless grief which deads my life, yet knows
not now to kill,
Go seek that hapless tomb, which if ye hap to
find,
Salute the stones, that keep the lines, that held
so good a mind. 40

1593. *Fulke Greville, Lord Brooke.*

LYCIDAS

Yet once more, O ye Laurels, and once more
Ye Myrtles brown, with Ivy never-sear,
I com to pluck your Berries harsh and crude,
And with forc'd fingers rude,
Shatter your leaves before the mellowing year.
Bitter constraint, and sad occasion dear,
Compels me to disturb your season due;
For Lycidas is dead, dead ere his prime,
Young Lycidas, and hath not left his peer:
Who would not sing for Lycidas? he knew 10
Himself to sing, and build the lofty rhyme.
He must not flote upon his watry bier
Unwept, and welter to the parching wind,
Without the meed of some melodious tear.
Begin, then, Sisters of the sacred well,
That from beneath the seat of Jove doth spring;
Begin, and somewhat loudly sweep the string.
Hence with denial vain, and coy excuse,
So may some gentle Muse
With lucky words favour my destin'd Urn, 20
And as he passes turn,
And bid fair peace be to my sable shrowd!
For we were nurst upon the self-same hill,
Fed the same flock, by fountain, shade, and rill.
Together both, ere the high Lawns appear'd

Under the opening eye-lids of the morn,
We drove a-field, and both together heard
What time the Gray-fly winds her sultry horn,
Batt'ning our flocks with the fresh dews of night,
Oft till the Star that rose, at Ev'ning, bright 30
Toward Heav'ns descent had slop'd his westering
wheel.
Mean while the Rural ditties were not mute,
Temper'd to th'Oaten Flute;
Rough Satyrs danc'd, and Fauns with clov'n heel,
From the glad sound would not be absent long,
And old Damœtas lov'd to hear our song.
But O the heavy change, now thou art gone,
Now thou art gone, and never must return!
Thee Shepherd, thee the Woods, and desert
Caves,
With wilde Thyme and the gadding Vine
o'regrown, 40
And all their echoes mourn.
The Willows, and the Hazle Copses green,
Shall now no more be seen,
Fanning their joyous Leaves to thy soft lays.
As killing as the Canker to the Rose,
Or Taint-worm to the weanling Herds that graze,
Or Frost to Flowers, that their gay wardrobe
wear,
When first the White thorn blows;
Such, Lycidas, thy loss to Shepherds ear.
Where were ye, Nymphs, when the remorseless
deep 50
Clos'd o'er the head of your lov'd Lycidas?
For neither were ye playing on the steep,

Where your old Bards, the famous Druids lie,
Nor on the shaggy top of Mona high,
Nor yet where Deva spreads her wisard stream:
Ay me, I fondly dream!
Had ye bin there—for what could that have done?
What could the Muse her self that Orpheus bore,
The Muse her self, for her inchanting son
Whom Universal nature did lament, 60
When by the rout that made the hideous roar,
His gory visage down the stream was sent,
Down the swift Hebrus to the Lesbian shore?
Alas! What boots it with uncessant care
To tend the homely slighted Shepherds trade,
And strictly meditate the thankless Muse,
Were it not better done as others use,
To sport with Amaryllis in the shade,
Or with the tangles of Neæra's hair?
Fame is the spur that the clear spirit doth
raise 70
(That last infirmity of Noble mind)
To scorn delights, and live laborious dayes;
But the fair Guerdon when we hope to find,
And think to burst out into sudden blaze,
Comes the blind Fury with th'abhorréd shears,
And slits the thin spun life. But not the praise,
Phœbus repli'd, and touch'd my trembling ears;
Fame is no plant that grows on mortal soil,
Nor in the glistering foil
Set off to th'world, nor in broad rumour lies, 80
But lives and spreds aloft by those pure eyes,
And perfet witness of all judging Jove;
As he pronounces lastly on each deed,

Of so much fame in Heav'n expect thy meed.
O fountain Arethuse, and thou honour'd flood,
Smooth-sliding Mincius, crown'd with vocal reeds,
That strain I heard was of a higher mood:
But now my Oat proceeds,
And listens to the Herald of the Sea
That came in Neptune's plea, 90
He ask'd the Waves, and ask'd the Fellon winds,
What hard mishap hath doom'd this gentle swain?
And question'd every gust of rugged wings
That blows from off each beakéd Promontory,
They knew not of his story,
And sage Hippotades their answer brings,
That not a blast was from his dungeon stray'd,
The Ayr was calm, and on the level brine,
Sleek Panope with all her sisters play'd.
It was that fatal and perfidious Bark 100
Built in th'eclipse, and rigg'd with curses dark,
That sunk so low that sacred head of thine.
Next Camus, reverend Sire, went footing slow,
His Mantle hairy, and his Bonnet sedge,
Inwrought with figures dim, and on the edge
Like to that sanguine flower inscrib'd with woe.
Ah! Who hath reft (quoth he) my dearest pledge?
Last came, and last did go,
The Pilot of the Galilean lake,
Two massy Keys he bore of metals twain, 110
(The Golden opes, the Iron shuts amain)

He shook his Miter'd locks, and stern bespake,
How well could I have spar'd for thee, young
 swain,
Anow of such as for their bellies sake,
Creep and intrude, and climb into the fold?
Of other care they little reck'ning make,
Than how to scramble at the shearers feast,
And shove away the worthy bidden guest.
Blind mouths! that scarce themselves know
 how to hold
A Sheep-hook, or have learn'd ought else the
 least 120
That to the faithful Herdman's art belongs!
What recks it them? What need they? They
 are sped;
And when they list, their lean and flashly songs
Grate on their scrannel Pipes of wretched straw;
The hungry Sheep look up, and are not fed,
But swoln with wind, and the rank mist they
 draw,
Rot inwardly, and foul contagion spread:
Besides what the grim Woolf with privy paw
Daily devours apace, and nothing sed,
But that two-handed engine at the door 130
Stands ready to smite once, and smite no more.
 Return Alpheus, the dread voice is past,
That shrunk thy streams; return Sicilian Muse,
And call the Vales, and bid them hither cast
Their bels, and flowrets of a thousand hues.
Ye valleys low where the mild whispers use,
Of shades and wanton winds, and gushing
 brooks,
On whose fresh lap the swart Star sparely looks,

Throw hither all your quaint enamell'd eyes,
That on the green terf suck the honied
showers, 140
And purple all the ground with vernal flowers.
Bring the rathe Primrose that forsaken dies.
The tufted Crow-toe, and pale Jessamine,
The white Pink, and the Pansy freakt with jet,
The glowing Violet.
The Musk-rose, and the well attir'd Woodbine.
With Cowslips wan that hang the pensive head,
And every flower that sad embroidery wears:
Bid Amaranthus all his beauty shed,
And Daffadillies fill their cups with tears, 150
To strew the Laureat Hearse where Lycid lies.
For so to interpose a little ease,
Let our frail thoughts dally with false surmise.
Ay me! Whilst thee the shores, and sounding
Seas
Wash far away, where ere thy bones are hurl'd,
Whether beyond the stormy Hebrides,
Where thou perhaps under the whelming tide
Visit'st the bottom of the monstrous world;
Or whether thou to our moist vows deni'd,
Sleep'st by the fable of Bellerus old, 160
Where the great vision of the guarded Mount
Looks toward Namancos and Bayona's hold;
Look homeward Angel now, and melt with
ruth.
And, O ye Dolphins, waft the hapless youth.
Weep no more, woful Shepherds weep no more,
For Lycidas your sorrow is not dead,
Sunk though he be beneath the wat'ry floor,
So sinks the day-star in the Ocean bed,

And yet anon repairs his drooping head,
And tricks his beams, and with new spangled
Ore, 170
Flames in the forehead of the morning sky:
So Lycidas sunk low, but mounted high,
Through the dear might of him that walk'd the
waves
Where other groves, and other streams along,
With Nectar pure his oozy Locks he laves,
And hears the unexpressive nuptial Song,
In the blest Kingdoms meek of joy and love.
There entertain him all the Saints above,
In solemn troops, and sweet Societies
That sing, and singing in their glory move, 180
And wipe the tears for ever from his eyes.
Now, Lycidas, the Shepherds weep no more;
Hence forth thou art the Genius of the shore,
In thy large recompense, and shalt be good
To all that wander in that perilous flood.
Thus sang the uncouth Swain to th' oaks and
rills,
While the still morn went out with Sandals gray,
He touch'd the tender stops of various Quills,
With eager thought warbling his Doric lay:
And now the Sun had stretch'd out all the
hills, 190
And now was dropt into the Western bay;
At last he rose, and twitch'd his Mantle blue:
To-morrow to fresh Woods, and Pastures new.

1638. *John Milton.*

JOHN MILTON AT THE AGE OF TWELVE

ON THE DEATH OF THOMSON

In yonder grave a Druid lies,
  Where slowly winds the stealing wave;
The year's best sweets shall duteous rise
  To deck its poet's sylvan grave. 4

In yon deep bed of whispering reeds
  His airy harp shall now be laid,
That he, whose heart in sorrow bleeds,
  May love through life the soothing shade. 8

Then maids and youths shall linger here,
  And while its sounds at distance swell,
Shall sadly seem in Pity's ear
  To hear the woodland pilgrim's knell. 12

Remembrance oft shall haunt the shore
  When Thames in summer wreaths is drest,
And oft suspend the dashing oar,
  To bid his gentle spirit rest. 16

And oft, as ease and health retire
  To breezy lawn, or forest deep,
The friend shall view yon whitening spire,
  And 'mid the varied landscape weep. 20

But thou, who own'st that earthy bed,
  Ah! what will every dirge avail;
Or tears, which love and pity shed,
  That mourn beneath the gliding sail? 24

Yet lives there one whose heedless eye
  Shall scorn thy pale shrine glimmering near?
With him, sweet bard, may fancy die,
  And joy desert the blooming year. 28

But thou, lorn stream, whose sullen tide
  No sedge-crowned sisters now attend,
Now waft me from the green hill's side
  Whose cold turf hides the buried friend! 32

And see—the fairy valleys fade;
  Dun night has veiled the solemn view!
Yet once again, dear parted shade,
  Meek Nature's child, again adieu! 36

Thy genial meads, assigned to bless
  Thy life, shall mourn thy early doom;
There hinds and shepherd-girls shall dress
  With simple hands thy rural tomb. 40

Long, long, thy stone and pointed clay
  Shall melt the musing Briton's eyes:
O vales and wild woods! shall he say,
  In yonder grave your Druid lies! 44

1749. *William Collins.*

ELEGY ON CAPTAIN MATTHEW HENDERSON

O Death! thou tyrant fell and bloody!
The meikle Devil wi' a woodie
Haurl thee hame to his black smiddie
O'er hurcheon hides,
And like stock-fish come o'er his studdie
Wi' thy auld sides! 6

He 's gane, he 's gane! he 's frae us torn,
The ae best fellow e'er was born!
Thee, Matthew, Nature's sel' shall mourn
By wood and wild,
Where, haply, pity strays forlorn,
Frae man exiled. 12

Ye hills, near neebors o' the starns,
That proudly cock your cresting cairns!
Ye cliffs, the haunts of sailing yearns,
Where echo slumbers!
Come join ye, Nature's sturdiest bairns,
My wailing numbers! 18

Mourn, ilka grove the cushat kens!
Ye hazelly shaws and briery dens!

Ye burnies, wimplin' down your glens,
    Wi' toddlin' din,
Or foaming, strang, wi' hasty stens,
    Frae lin to lin! 24

Mourn, little harebells o'er the lea,
Ye stately foxgloves fair to see;
Ye woodbines hanging bonnilie
    In scented bowers;
Ye roses on your thorny tree,
    The first o' flowers! 30

At dawn, when every grassy blade
Droops with a diamond at his head,
At even, when beans their fragrance shed,
    I' the rustling gale;
Ye maukins whiddin through the glade,
    Come join my wail. 36

Mourn, ye wee songsters o' the wood;
Ye grouse that crap the heather bud;
Ye curlews calling through a clud;
    Ye whistling plover;
And mourn, ye whirring paitrick brood;
    He 's gane forever! 42

Mourn, sooty coots, and speckled teals;
Ye fisher herons, watching eels;
Ye duck and drake, wi' airy wheels
    Circling the lake;
Ye bitterns, till the quagmire reels,
    Rair for his sake. 48

Mourn, clamoring craiks, at close o' day,
'Mang fields o' flowering clover gay;
And when you wing your annual way
Frae our cauld shore,
Tell thae far warlds wha lies in clay,
Wham we deplore. 54

Ye houlets, frae your ivy bower,
In some auld tree, or eldritch tower,
What time the moon, wi' silent glower,
Sets up her horn,
Wail thro' the dreary midnight hour
Till waukrife morn. 60

O rivers, forests, hills and plains!
Oft have ye heard my canty strains:
But now, what else for me remains
But tales of wo?
And frae my een the drapping rains
Maun ever flow. 66

Mourn, Spring, thou darling of the year!
Ilk cowslip cup shall kep a tear:
Thou, Simmer, while each corny spear
Shoots up its head,
Thy gay green flowery tresses shear,
For him that 's dead! 72

Thou Autumn, wi' thy yellow hair,
In grief thy sallow mantle tear!
Thou, Winter, hurling through the air

The roaring blast,
Wide o'er the naked world declare
The worth we 've lost. 78

Mourn him, thou sun, great source of light!
Mourn, empress of the silent night!
And you, ye twinkling starnies bright,
My Matthew mourn!
For thro' your orbs he 's ta'en his flight,
Ne'er to return. 84

O Henderson, the man! the brother!
And art thou gone, and gone forever?
And hast thou crost that unknown river,
Life's dreary bound?
Like thee where shall I find another,
The world around? 90

Go to your sculptured tombs, ye great,
In a' the tinsel trash o' state!
But by thy honest turf I 'll wait,
Thou man of worth!
And weep the ae best fellow's fate
E'er lay in earth. 96

1793. *Robert Burns.*

THOUGHTS

After a visit to the grave of Burns

Too frail to keep the lofty vow
That must have followed when his brow
Was wreathed—"The Vision" tells us how—
With holly spray,
He faltered, drifted to and fro,
And passed away. 6

Well might such thoughts, dear Sister, throng
Our minds when, lingering all too long,
Over the grave of Burns we hung
In social grief—
Indulged as if it were a wrong
To seek relief. 12

But, leaving each unquiet theme
Where gentlest judgments may misdeem,
And prompt to welcome every gleam
Of good and fair,
Let us beside this limpid Stream
Breathe hopeful air. 18

Enough of sorrow, wreck, and blight;
Think rather of those moments bright
When to the consciousness of right

His course was true,
When Wisdom prospered in his sight,
And virtue grew. 24

Yes, freely let our hearts expand,
Freely as in youth's season bland,
When side by side, his Book in hand,
We wont to stray,
Our pleasure varying at command
Of each sweet Lay. 30

How oft inspired must he have trod
These pathways, yon far-stretching road!
There lurks his home; in that Abode,
With mirth elate,
Or in his nobly-pensive mood,
The Rustic sate. 36

Proud thoughts that Image overawes,
Before it humbly let us pause,
And ask of Nature, from what cause,
And by what rules
She trained her Burns to win applause
That shames the Schools. 42

Through busiest street and loneliest glen
Are felt the flashes of his pen;
He rules 'mid winter snows, and when
Bees fill their hives;
Deep in the general heart of men
His power survives. 48

What need of fields in some far clime
Where Heroes, Sages, Bards sublime,
And all that fetched the flowing rhyme
  From genuine springs,
Shall dwell together till old Time
  Folds up his wings? 54

Sweet Mercy! to the gates of Heaven
This Minstrel lead, his sins forgiven;
The rueful conflict, the heart riven
  With vain endeavour,
And memory of Earth's bitter leaven,
  Effaced for ever. 60

But why to Him confine the prayer,
When kindred thoughts and yearnings bear
On the frail heart the purest share
  With all that live?—
The best of what we do and are,
  Just God, forgive! 66

1803. 1845. *William Wordsworth.*

BURNS

Wild rose of Alloway! my thanks;
 Thou 'mind'st me of that autumn noon
When first we met upon "the banks
 And braes o' bonny Doon." 4

Like thine, beneath the thorn-tree's bough,
 My sunny hour was glad and brief;

We 've crossed the winter sea, and thou
  Art withered—flower and leaf. 8

And will not thy death-doom be mine—
  The doom of all things wrought of clay?
And withered my life's leaf like thine,
  Wild rose of Alloway? 12

Not so his memory for whose sake
  My bosom bore thee far and long—
His, who a humbler flower could make
  Immortal as his song, 16

The memory of Burns—a name
  That calls, when brimmed her festal cup,
A nation's glory and her shame,
  In silent sadness up. 20

A nation's glory—be the rest
  Forgot—she 's canonized his mind,
And it is joy to speak the best
  We may of humankind. 24

I 've stood beside the cottage bed
  Where the bard-peasant first drew breath;
A straw-thatched roof above his head,
  A straw-wrought couch beneath. 28

And I have stood beside the pile,
  His monument—that tells to Heaven
The homage of earth's proudest isle
  To that bard-peasant given. 32

Bid thy thoughts hover o'er that spot,
  Boy-minstrel, in thy dreaming hour;
And know, however low his lot,
  A poet's pride and power; 36

The pride that lifted Burns from earth,
  The power that gave a child of song
Ascendency o'er rank and birth,
  The rich, the brave, the strong; 40

And if despondency weigh down
  Thy spirit's fluttering pinions then,
Despair—thy name is written on
  The roll of common men. 44

There have been loftier themes than his,
  And longer scrolls, and louder lyres,
And lays lit up with Poesy's
  Purer and holier fires: 48

Yet read the names that know not death;
  Few nobler ones than Burns are there;
And few have won a greener wreath
  Than that which binds his hair. 52

His is that language of the heart
  In which the answering heart would speak,
Thought, word, that bids the warm tear start,
  Or the smile light the cheek; 56

And his that music to whose tone
  The common pulse of man keeps time,

In cot or castle's mirth or moan,
  In cold or sunny clime. 60

And who has heard his song, nor knelt
  Before its spell with willing knee,
And listened and believed, and felt
  The poet's mastery. 64

O'er the mind's sea, in calm and storm,
  O'er the heart's sunshine and its showers,
O'er Passion's moments, bright and warm,
  O'er Reason's dark, cold hours; 68

On fields where brave men "die or do,"
  In halls where rings the banquet's mirth,
Where mourners weep, where lovers woo,
  From throne to cottage hearth? 72

What sweet tears dim the eye unshed,
  What wild vows falter on the tongue,
When "Scots wha hae wi' Wallace bled,"
  Or "Auld Lang Syne," is sung! 76

Pure hopes that lift the soul above,
  Come with his Cotter's hymn of praise,
And dreams of youth, and truth, and love,
  With "Logan's" banks and braes. 80

And when he breathes his master-lay
  Of Alloway's witch-haunted wall,
All passions in our frames of clay
  Come thronging at his call. 84

Imagination's world of air,
  And our own world, its gloom and glee,
Wit, pathos, poetry, are there,
  And death's sublimity. 88

And Burns—though brief the race he ran,
  Though rough and dark the path he trod—
Lived, died, in form and soul a man,
  The image of his God. 92

Through care, and pain, and want, and woe,
  With wounds that only death could heal,
Tortures—the poor alone can know,
  The proud alone can feel; 96

He kept his honesty and truth,
  His independent tongue and pen,
And moved, in manhood as in youth,
  Pride of his fellow-men. 100

Strong sense, deep feeling, passions strong,
  A hate of tyrant and of knave,
A love of right, a scorn of wrong,
  Of coward and of slave; 104

A kind, true heart, a spirit high,
  That could not fear and would not bow,
Were written in his manly eye
  And on his manly brow. 108

Praise to the bard! his words are driven,
  Like flower-seeds by the far winds sown.

Where'er beneath the sky of heaven,
The birds of fame have flown. 112

Praise to the man! a nation stood
Beside his coffin with wet eyes,
Her brave, her beautiful, her good,
As when a loved one dies. 116

And still, as on his funeral-day,
Men stand his cold earth-couch around,
With the mute homage that we pay
To consecrated ground. 120

And consecrated ground it is,
The last, the hallowed home of one
Who lives upon all memories,
Though with the buried gone. 124

Such graves as his are pilgrim-shrines,
Shrines to no code or creed confined—
The Delphian vales, the Palestines,
The Meccas of the mind. 128

Sages, with Wisdom's garland wreathed,
Crowned kings, and mitred priests of power,
And warriors with their bright swords sheathed,
The mightiest of the hour; 132

And lowlier names, whose humble home
Is lit by Fortune's dimmer star,
Are there—o'er wave and mountain come,
From countries near and far; 136

Pilgrims, whose wandering feet have pressed
  The Switzer's snow, the Arab's sand,
Or trod the piled leaves of the West,
  My own green forest-land. 140

All ask the cottage of his birth,
  Gaze on the scenes he loved and sung,
And gather feelings not of earth
  His fields and streams among. 144

They linger by the Doon's low trees,
  And pastoral Nith, and wooded Ayr,
And round thy sepulchres, Dumfries!
  The Poët's tomb is there. 148

But what to them the Sculptor's art,
  His funeral columns, wreaths, and urns?
Wear they not graven on the heart
  The name of Robert Burns? 152

1822. *Fitz-Greene Halleck.*

THE OLD FAMILIAR FACES

Where are they gone, the old familiar faces?

I HAVE had playmates, I have had companions,
In my days of childhood, in my joyful school-
    days;
All, all are gone, the old familiar faces. 3

I have been laughing, I have been carousing,
Drinking late, sitting late, with my bosom
cronies;
All, all are gone, the old familiar faces. 6

I loved a Love once, fairest among women:
Closed are her doors on me, I must not see her,—
All, all are gone, the old familiar faces. 9

I have a friend, a kinder friend has no man;
Like an ingrate, I left my friend abruptly;
Left him, to muse on the old familiar faces. 12

Ghost-like I paced round the haunts of my child-
hood;
Earth seemed a desert I was bound to traverse,
Seeking to find the old familiar faces. 15

Friend of my bosom, thou more than a brother,
Why wert not thou born in my father's dwelling?
So might we talk of the old familiar faces. 18

For some they have died, and some they have
left me,
And some are taken from me; all are departed;
All, all are gone, the old familiar faces. 21

1798. *Charles Lamb.*

HESTER

WHEN maidens such as Hester die,
Their place ye may not well supply,
Though ye among a thousand try
With vain endeavour. 4

A month or more hath she been dead,
Yet cannot I by force be led
To think upon the wormy bed,
And her together. 8

A springy motion in her gait,
A rising step, did indicate
Of pride and joy no common rate,
That flush'd her spirit: 12

I know not by what name beside
I shall it call: if 't was not pride,
It was a joy to that allied,
She did inherit. 16

Her parents held the Quaker rule,
Which doth the human feeling cool;
But she was train'd in Nature's school;
Nature had blest her. 20

A waking eye, a prying mind;
A heart that stirs, is hard to bind;
A hawk's keen sight ye cannot blind;
Ye could not Hester. 24

My sprightly neighbour! gone before
To that unknown and silent shore,
Shall we not meet, as heretofore,
Some summer morning, 28

When from thy cheerful eyes a ray
Hath struck a bliss upon the day,
A bliss that would not go away,
A sweet forewarning? 32

1803. *Charles Lamb.*

TO THE SISTER OF ELIA

Comfort thee, O thou mourner, yet awhile!
Again shall Elia's smile
Refresh thy heart, where heart can ache no more.
What is it we deplore? 4

He leaves behind him, freed from griefs and years,
Far worthier things than tears.
The love of friends without a single foe:
Unequalled lot below! 8

His gentle soul, his genius, these are thine;
For these dost thou repine?

He may have left the lowly walks of men;
  Left them he has; what then? 12

Are not his footsteps followed by the eyes
  Of all the good and wise?
Tho' the warm day is over, yet they seek
  Upon the lofty peak 16

Of his pure mind the roseate light that glows
  O'er death's perennial snows.
Behold him! from the region of the blest
  He speaks: he bids thee rest. 20

1837. *Walter Savage Landor.*

MEMORIAL VERSES

GOETHE in Weimar sleeps, and Greece,
Long since, saw Byron's struggle cease.
But one such death remained to come;
The last poetic voice is dumb—
We stand to-day by Wordsworth's tomb.

When Byron's eyes were shut in death,
We bowed our head and held our breath.
He taught us little; but our soul
Had *felt* him like the thunder's roll.
With shivering heart the strife we saw 10
Of passion with eternal law;
And yet with reverential awe
We watched the fount of fiery life
Which served for that Titanic strife.

When Goethe's death was told, we said:
Sunk, then, is Europe's sagest head.
Physician of the iron age,
Goethe has done his pilgrimage.
He took the suffering human race,
He read each wound, each weakness clear; 20
And struck his finger on the place,
And said: *Thou ailest here, and here!*
He looked on Europe's dying hour
Of fitful dream and feverish power;
His eye plunged down the weltering strife,
The turmoil of expiring life—
He said: *The end is everywhere,*
Art still has truth, take refuge there!
And he was happy, if to know
Causes of things, and far below 30
His feet to see the lurid flow
Of terror, and insane distress,
And headlong fate, be happiness.

And Wordsworth!—Ah, pale ghosts, rejoice!
For never has such soothing voice
Been to your shadowy world conveyed,
Since erst, at morn, some wandering shade
Heard the clear song of Orpheus come
Through Hades, and the mournful gloom.
Wordsworth has gone from us—and ye, 40
Ah, may ye feel his voice as we!
He too upon a wintry clime
Had fallen—on this iron time
Of doubts, disputes, distractions, fears.

He found us when the age had bound
Our souls in its benumbing round;
He spoke, and loosed our heart in tears.
He laid us as we lay at birth
On the cool flowery lap of earth,
Smiles broke from us and we had ease; 50
The hills were round us, and the breeze
Went o'er the sun-lit fields again;
Our foreheads felt the wind and rain.
Our youth returned; for there was shed
On spirits that had long been dead,
Spirits dried up and closely furled,
The freshness of the early world.

Ah! since dark days still bring to light
Man's prudence and man's fiery might,
Time may restore us in his course 60
Goethe's sage mind and Byron's force;
But where will Europe's latter hour
Again find Wordsworth's healing power?
Others will teach us how to dare,
And against fear our breast to steel;
Others will strengthen us to bear—
But who, ah! who, will make us feel?
The cloud of mortal destiny,
Others will front it fearlessly—
But who, like him, will put it by? 70

Keep fresh the grass upon his grave
O Rotha, with thy living wave!
Sing him thy best! for few or none
Hears thy voice right, now he is gone.

1850. *Matthew Arnold.*

ON THE DEATH OF MR. WILLIAM HERVEY

It was a dismal and a fearful night,
Scarce could the morn drive on the unwilling light,
When sleep, death's image, left my troubled breast,
By something liker death possessed.
My eyes with tears did uncommanded flow,
And on my soul hung the dull weight
Of some intolerable fate.
What bell was that? Ah me! too much I know. 8

My sweet companion, and my gentle peer,
Why hast thou left me thus unkindly here,
Thy end for ever, and my life, to moan?
O, thou hast left me all alone!
Thy soul and body, when Death's agony
Besieged around thy noble heart,
Did not with more reluctance part,
Than I, my dearest friend! do part from thee. 16

My dearest friend, would I had died for thee!
Life and this world henceforth will tedious be.

Nor shall I know hereafter what to do,
  If once my griefs prove tedious too.
Silent and sad I walk about all day,
  As sullen ghosts stalk speechless by
  Where their hid treasures lie;
Alas! my treasure 's gone! why do I stay? 24

He was my friend, the truest friend on earth;
A strong and mighty influence joined our birth;
Nor did we envy the most sounding name
  By friendship given of old to fame.
None but his brethren he and sisters knew
  Whom the kind youth preferred to me;
  And even in that we did agree,
For much above myself I loved them too. 32

Say, for you saw us, ye immortal lights,
How oft unwearied have we spent the nights,
Till the Ledaean stars, so famed for love,
  Wondered at us from above!
We spent them not in toys, in lusts, or wine;
  But search of deep Philosophy,
  Wit, Eloquence, and Poetry,
Arts which I loved, for they, my friend, were
    thine. 40

Ye fields of Cambridge, our dear Cambridge,
    say
Have ye not seen us walking every day?
Was there a tree about which did not know
  The love betwixt us two?

Henceforth, ye gentle trees for ever fade;
  Or your sad branches thicker join,
  And into darksome shades combine,
Dark as the grave wherein my friend is laid! 48

Henceforth, no learned youths beneath you sing,
Till all the tuneful birds to your boughs they
    bring;
No tuneful birds play with their wonted cheer,
  And called the learned youths to hear;
No whistling winds through the glad branches
    fly:
  But all, with sad solemnity,
  Mute and unmovèd be,
Mute as the grave wherein my friend does lie. 56

To him my Muse made haste with every strain,
Whilst it was new and warm yet from the brain;
He loved my worthless rhymes, and, like a friend,
  Would find out something to commend.
Hence now, my Muse! thou canst not me
    delight:
  Be this my latest verse,
  With which I now adorn his hearse;
And this my grief, without thy help, shall
    write. 64

Had I a wreath of bays about my brow,
I should contemn that flourishing honour now;
Condemn it to the fire, and joy to hear
  It rage and crackle there.

On the Death of Mr. William Hervey

Instead of bays, crown with sad cypress me;
  Cypress, which tombs does beautify:
  Not Phœbus grieved so much as I,
For him who first was made that mournful
    tree. 72

Large was his soul: as large a soul as e'er
Submitted to inform a body here;
High as the place 't was shortly in heaven to
    have,
  But low and humble as his grave:
So high that all the virtues there did come,
  As to their chiefest seat
  Conspicuous and great:
So low, that for me too it made a room. 80

He scorned this busy world below, and all
That we, mistaken mortals! pleasure call;
Was filled with innocent gallantry and truth,
  Triumphant o'er the sins of youth.
He, like the stars, to which he now is gone,
  That shine with beams like flame,
  Yet burn not with the same,
Had all the light of youth, of the fire none. 88

Knowledge he only sought, and so soon caught,
As if for him knowledge had rather sought:
Nor did more learning ever crowded lie
  In such a short mortality.
Whene'er the skilful youth discoursed or writ,
  Still did the notions throng
  About his eloquent tongue,
Nor could his ink flow faster than his wit. 96

So strong a wit did Nature to him frame,
As all things but his judgment overcame;
His judgment like the heavenly moon did show.
  Tempering that mighty sea below.
Oh! had he lived in Learning's world, what
    bound
  Would have been able to control
  His overpowering soul!
We 've lost in him arts that not yet are
    found. 104

His mirth was the pure spirits of various wit,
Yet never did his God or friends forget;
And, when deep talk and wisdom came in view,
  Retired and gave to them their due:
For the rich help of books he always took,
  Though his own searching mind before
  Was so with notions written o'er
As if wise Nature had made that her book. 112

So many virtues joined in him, as we
Can scarce pick here and there in history;
More than old writers' practice e'er could reach;
  As much as they could ever teach.
These did Religion, Queen of Virtues! sway:
  And all their sacred motions steer,
  Just like the first and highest sphere,
Which wheels about, and turns all heaven one
    way. 120

With as much zeal, devotion, piety,
He always lived, as other saints do die.

Still with his soul severe account he kept,
  Weeping all debts out ere he slept:
Then down in peace and innocence he lay,
  Like the sun's laborious light,
  Which still in water sets at night,
Unsullied with his journey of the day. 128

Wondrous young man! why wert thou made so
    good,
To be snatched hence ere better understood?
Snatched before half of thee enough was seen!
  Thou ripe, and yet thy life but green!
Nor could thy friends take their last sad
    farewell;
  But danger and infectious death
  Maliciously seized on that breath
Where life, spirit, pleasure, always used to
    dwell. 136

But happy thou, ta'en from this frantic age,
Where ignorance and hypocrisy does rage!
A fitter time for heaven no soul ere chose,
  The place now only free from those.
There 'mong the blest thou dost for ever shine,
  And wheresoe'er thou cast'st thy view,
  Upon that white and radiant crew,
Seest not a soul clothed with more light than
    thine. 144

And if the glorious saints cease not to know
Their wretched friends who fight with life below,

Thy flame to me does still the same abide,
Only more pure and rarified.
There, whilst immortal hymns thou dost rehearse,
Thou dost with holy pity see
Our dull and earthly poesy,
Where grief and misery can be joined with verse. 152

1656. *Abraham Cowley.*

THYRSIS

A Monody, *to commemorate the author's friend,* Arthur Hugh Clough, *who died at Florence, 1861*

How changed is here each spot man makes or fills!
In the two Hinkseys nothing keeps the same;
The village street its haunted mansion lacks,
And from the sign is gone Sibylla's name,
And from the roofs the twisted chimney-stacks—
Are ye too changed, ye hills?
See, 't is no foot of unfamiliar men
To-night from Oxford up your pathway strays!
Here came I often, often, in old days—
Thyrsis and I; we still had Thyrsis then. 10

Runs it not here, the track by Childsworth
Farm,
Past the high wood, to where the elm-tree
crowns
The hill behind whose ridge the sunset
flames?
The signal-elm, that looks on Ilsley Downs,
The Vale, the three lone weirs, the youthful
Thames?—
This winter-eve is warm,
Humid the air! leafless, yet soft as spring,
The tender purple spray on copse and
briars!
And that sweet city with her dreaming spires,
She needs not June for beauty's heightening. 20

Lovely all times she lies, lovely to-night!—
Only, methinks, some loss of habit's power
Befalls me wandering through this upland
dim.
Once pass'd I blindfold here, at any hour;
Now seldom come I, since I came with him.
That single elm-tree bright
Against the west—I miss it! is it gone?
We prized it dearly; while it stood, we said,
Our friend, the Gipsy-Scholar, was not dead;
While the tree lived, he in these fields
lived on. 30

Too rare, too rare, grow now my visits here,
But once I knew each field, each flower, each
stick;

And with the country-folk acquaintance made
By barn in threshing-time, by new-built rick.
Here, too, our shepherd-pipes we first assay'd.
Ah me! this many a year
My pipe is lost, my shepherd's holiday!
Needs must I lose them, needs with heavy heart
Into the world and wave of men depart;
But Thyrsis of his own will went away. 40

It irk'd him to be here, he could not rest.
He loved each simple joy the country yields,
He loved his mates; but yet he could not keep,
For that a shadow lour'd on the fields,
Here with the shepherds and the silly sheep.
Some life of men unblest
He knew, which made him droop, and fill'd his head.
He went; his piping took a troubled sound
Of storms that rage outside our happy happy ground;
He could not wait their passing, he is dead. 50

So, some tempestuous morn in early June,
When the year's primal burst of bloom is o'er,
Before the roses and the longest day—
When garden-walks and all the grassy floor

With blossoms red and white of fallen May
And chestnut-flowers are strewn—
So have I heard the cuckoo's parting cry,
From the wet-field, through the vext garden-trees,
Come with the volleying rain and tossing breeze:
The bloom is gone, and with the bloom go I! 60

Too quick despairer, wherefore wilt thou go?
Soon will the high Midsummer pomps come on,
Soon will the musk carnations break and swell,
Soon shall we have gold-dusted snapdragon,
Sweet-William with his homely cottage-smell,
And stocks in fragrant blow;
Roses that down the alleys shine afar,
And open, jasmine-muffled lattices,
And groups under the dreaming garden-trees,
And the full moon, and the white evening-star. 70

He harkens not! light comer, he is flown!
What matters it? next year he will return,
And we shall have him in the sweet spring-days,
With whitening hedges, and uncrumpling fern,
And blue-bells trembling by the forest-ways,
And scent of hay new-mown.

But Thyrsis never more we swains shall see;
See him come back, and cut a smoother reed,
And blow a strain the world at last shall heed—
For Time, not Corydon, hath conquer'd thee! 80

Alack, for Corydon no rival now!—
But when Sicilian shepherds lost a mate,
Some good survivor with his flute would go,
Piping a ditty sad for Bion's fate;
And cross the unpermitted ferry's flow,
And relax Pluto's brow,
And make leap up with joy the beauteous head
Of Proserpine, among whose crowned hair
Are flowers first open'd on Sicilian air,
And flute his friend, like Orpheus, from the dead. 90

O easy access to the hearer's grace
When Dorian shepherds sang to Proserpine!
For she herself had trod Sicilian fields,
She knew the Dorian water's gush divine,
She knew each lily white which Enna yields,
Each rose with blushing face;
She loved the Dorian pipe, the Dorian strain.
But ah, of our poor Thames she never heard!
Her foot the Cumner cowslips never stirr'd;
And we should tease her with our plaint in vain! 100

Well! wind-dispersed and vain the words will be,
Yet, Thyrsis, let me give my grief its hour
In the old haunt, and find our tree-topp'd hill!
Who, if not I, for questing here hath power?
I know the wood which hides the daffodil,
I know the Fyfield tree,
I know what white, what purple fritillaries
The grassy harvest of the river-fields,
Above by Ensham, down by Sandford, yields,
And what sedged brooks are Thames's tributaries; 110

I know these slopes; who knows them if not I?—
But many a dingle on the loved hill-side,
With thorns once studded, old, white-blossom'd trees,
Where thick the cowslips grew, and far descried
High tower'd the spikes of purple orchises,
Hath since our day put by
The coronals of that forgotten time;
Down each green bank hath gone the ploughboy's team,
And only in the hidden brookside gleam
Primroses, orphans of the flowery prime. 120

Where is the girl, who by the boatman's door,
Above the locks, above the boating throng,
Unmoor'd our skiff when through the Wytham flats,

Red loosestrife and blond meadow-sweet
among
And darting swallows and light water-gnats,
We track'd the shy Thames shore?
Where are the mowers, who, as the tiny swell
Of our boat passing heaved the river-grass,
Stood with suspended scythe to see us
pass?—
They all are gone, and thou art gone as
well! 130

Yes, thou art gone! and round me too the night
In ever-nearing circle weaves her shade.
I see her veil draw soft across the day,
I feel her slowly chilling breath invade
The cheek grown thin, the brown hair sprent
with gray;
I feel her finger light
Laid pausefully upon life's headlong train;—
The foot less prompt to meet the morning
dew,
The heart less bounding at emotion new,
And hope, once crush'd, less quick to spring
again. 140

And long the way appears, which seem'd so
short
To the less practised eye of sanguine youth;
And high the mountain-tops, in cloudy air,
The mountain-tops where is the throne of
Truth,

Tops in life's morning-sun so bright and
bare!
Unbreachable the fort
Of the long-batter'd world uplifts its wall;
And strange and vain the earthly turmoil
grows,
And near and real the charm of thy repose,
And night as welcome as a friend would
fall. 150

But hush! the upland hath a sudden loss
Of quiet!—Look, adown the dusk hill-side,
A troop of Oxford hunters going home,
As in old days, jovial and talking, ride!
From hunting with the Berkshire hounds
they come.
Quick! let me fly, and cross
Into yon farther field!—'T is done; and see,
Back'd by the sunset, which doth glorify
The orange and pale violet evening-sky,
Bare on its lonely ridge, the Tree! the
Tree! 160

I take the omen! Eve lets down her veil,
The white fog creeps from bush to bush
about,
The west unflushes, the high stars grow
bright,
And in the scatter'd farms the lights come out.
I cannot reach the signal-tree to-night,
Yet, happy omen, hail!

Hear it from thy broad lucent Arnovale
(For there thine earth-forgetting eyelids keep
The morningless and unawakening sleep
Under the flowery oleanders pale), 170

Hear it, O Thyrsis, still our tree is there!—
Ah, vain! These English fields, this upland dim,
These brambles pale with mist engarlanded,
That lone, sky-pointing tree, are not for him;
To a boon southern country he is fled,
And now in happier air,
Wandering with the great Mother's train divine
(And purer or more subtle soul than thee,
I trow, the mighty Mother doth not see)
Within a folding of the Apennine, 180

Thou hearest the immortal chants of old!—
Putting his sickle to the perilous grain
In the hot cornfield of the Phrygian king,
For thee the Lityerses-song again
Young Daphnis with his silver voice doth sing;
Sings his Sicilian fold,
His sheep, his hapless love, his blinded eyes—
And how a call celestial round him rang,
And heavenward from the fountain-brink he sprang,
And all the marvel of the golden skies. 190

There thou art gone, and me thou leavest here
Sole in these fields! yet will I not despair.
Despair I will not, while I yet descry
'Neath the mild canopy of English air
That lonely tree against the western sky.
Still, still these slopes, 't is clear,
Our Gipsy-Scholar haunts, outliving thee!
Fields where soft sheep from cages pull the hay,
Woods with anemonies in flower till May,
Know him a wanderer still; then why not me? 200

A fugitive and gracious light he seeks,
Shy to illumine; and I seek it too.
This does not come with houses or with gold,
With place, with honour, and a flattering crew;
'T is not in the world's market bought and sold—
But the smooth-slipping weeks
Drop by, and leave its seeker still untired;
Out of the heed of mortals he is gone,
He wends unfollow'd, he must house alone;
Yet on he fares, by his own heart inspired. 210

Thou too, O Thyrsis, on like quest wast bound;
Thou wanderedst with me for a little hour!
Men gave thee nothing; but this happy quest,
If men esteemed thee feeble, gave thee power,
If men procured thee trouble, gave thee rest.
And this rude Cumnor ground,

Its fir-topped Hurst, its farms, its quiet
fields,
Here cams't thou in thy jocund youthful
time,
Here was thine height of strength, thy
golden prime!
And still the haunt beloved a virtue yields. 220

What though the music of thy rustic flute
Kept not for long its happy, country tone;
Lost it too soon, and learnt a stormy note
Of men contention-tost, of men who groan,
Which task'd thy pipe too sore, and tired
thy throat—
It fail'd, and thou wast mute!
Yet hadst thou alway visions of our light,
And long with men of care thou couldst
not stay,
And soon thy foot resumed its wandering
way,
Left human haunt, and on alone till night. 230

Too rare, too rare, grow now my visits here!
'Mid city-noise, not, as with thee of yore,
Thyrsis! in reach of sheep-bells is my home.
—Then through the great town's harsh,
heart-wearying roar,
Let in thy voice a whisper often come,
To chase fatigue and fear:

Why faintest thou? I wonder'd till I died.
Roam on! The light we sought is shining still.
Dost thou ask proof? Our tree yet crowns the hill,
Our Scholar travels yet the loved hill-side. 240

1866. *Matthew Arnold.*

RUGBY CHAPEL

November, 1857

COLDLY, sadly descends
The autumn-evening. The field
Strewn with its dank yellow drifts
Of wither'd leaves, and the elms,
Fade into dimness apace,
Silent;—hardly a shout
From a few boys late at their play!
The lights come out in the street,
In the school-room windows;—but cold,
Solemn, unlighted, austere, 10
Through the gathering darkness, arise
The chapel-walls, in whose bound
Thou, my father! art laid.

There thou dost lie, in the gloom
Of the autumn evening. But ah!
That word, *gloom*, to my mind
Brings thee back, in the light

Of thy radiant vigour, again;
In the gloom of November we pass'd
Days not dark at thy side; 20
Seasons impair'd not the ray
Of thy buoyant cheerfulness clear.
Such thou wast! and I stand
In the autumn evening, and think
Of bygone autumns with thee.

Fifteen years have gone round
Since thou arosest to tread,
In the summer-morning, the road
Of death, at a call unforeseen,
Sudden. For fifteen years, 30
We who till then in thy shade
Rested as under the boughs
Of a mighty oak, have endured
Sunshine and rain as we might,
Bare, unshaded, alone,
Lacking the shelter of thee.

O strong soul, by what shore
Tarriest thou now? For that force,
Surely, has not been left vain!
Somewhere, surely, afar, 40
In the sounding labor-house vast
Of being, is practised that strength,
Zealous, beneficent, firm!

Yes, in some far-shining sphere,
Conscious or not of the past,

Still thou performest the word
Of the Spirit in whom thou dost live—
Prompt, unwearied, as here!
Still thou upraisest with zeal
The humble good from the ground, 50
Sternly repressest the bad!
Still, like a trumpet, dost rouse

Those who with half-open eyes
Tread the border-land dim
Twixt vice and virtue; reviv'st,
Succorest!—this was thy work,
This was thy life upon earth.

What is the course of the life
Of mortal men on the earth?—
Most men eddy about 60
Here and there—eat and drink,
Chatter and love and hate,
Gather and squander, are raised
Aloft, are hurl'd in the dust,
Striving blindly, achieving
Nothing; and then they die—
Perish;—and no one asks
Who or what they have been,
More than he asks what waves,
In the moonlit solitudes mild 70
Of the midmost Ocean, have swell'd,
Foam'd for a moment, and gone.

And there are some, whom a thirst
Ardent, unquenchable, fires,

Not with the crowd to be spent,
Not without aim to go round
In an eddy of purposeless dust,
Effort unmeaning and vain.
Ah yes! some of us strive
Not without action to die 80
Fruitless, but something to snatch
From dull oblivion, nor all
Glut the devouring grave!
We, we have chosen our path—
Path to a clear-purposed goal,
Path of advance!—but it leads
A long, steep journey, through sunk
Gorges, o'er mountains in snow.
Cheerful, with friends, we set forth—
Then on the height, comes the storm. 90
Thunder crashes from rock
To rock, the cataracts reply,
Lightnings dazzle our eyes.
Roaring torrents have breach'd
The track, the stream-bed descends
In the place where the wayfarer once
Planted his footstep—the spray
Boils o'er its borders! aloft
The unseen snow-beds dislodge
Their hanging ruin; alas, 100
Havoc is made in our train!
Friends, who set forth at our side,
Falter, are lost in the storm.
We, we only are left!
With frowning foreheads, with lips
Sternly compress'd, we strain on,

On—and at nightfall at last
Come to the end of our way,
To the lonely inn 'mid the rocks;
Where the gaunt and taciturn host 110
Stands on the threshold, the wind
Shaking his thin white hairs—
Holds his lantern to scan
Our storm-beat figures, and asks:
Whom in our party we bring?
Whom we have left in the snow?

Sadly we answer: We bring
Only ourselves! we lost
Sight of the rest in the storm.
Hardly ourselves we fought through, 120
Stripp'd, without friends, as we are.
Friends, companions, and train,
The avalanche swept from our side.

But thou would'st not *alone*
Be saved, my father! *alone*
Conquer and come to thy goal,
Leaving the rest in the wild.
We were weary, and we
Fearful, and we in our march
Fain to drop down and to die. 130
Still thou turnedst, and still
Beckonedst the trembler, and still
Gavest the weary thy hand.

If, in the paths of the world,
Stones might have wounded thy feet,

Toil or dejection have tried
Thy spirit, of that we saw
Nothing—to us thou wast still
Cheerful, and helpful, and firm!
Therefore to thee it was given 140
Many to save with thyself;
And, at the end of thy day,
O faithful shepherd! to come,
Bringing thy sheep in thy hand.
And through thee I believe
In the noble and great who are gone;
Pure souls honour'd and blest
By former ages, who else—
Such, so soulless, so poor,
Is the race of men whom I see— 150
Seem'd but a dream of the heart,
Seem'd but a cry of desire.
Yes! I believe that there lived
Others like thee in the past,
Not like the men of the crowd
Who all round me to-day
Bluster or cringe, and make life
Hideous, and arid, and vile;
But souls temper'd with fire,
Fervent, heroic, and good, 160
Helpers and friends of mankind.

Servants of God!—or sons
Shall I not call you? because
Not as servants ye knew
Your Father's innermost mind,
His, who unwillingly sees

One of his little ones lost—
Yours is the praise, if mankind
Hath not as yet in its march
Fainted, and fallen, and died! 170

See! In the rocks of the world
Marches the host of mankind,
A feeble, wavering line.
Where are they tending?—A God
Marshall'd them, gave them their goal.
Ah, but the way is so long!
Years they have been in the wild!
Sore thirst plagues them, the rocks,
Rising all round, overawe;
Factions divide them, their host 180
Threatens to break, to dissolve.
—Ah, keep, keep them combined!
Else, of the myriads who fill
That army, not one shall arrive;
Sole they shall stray; in the rocks
Stagger for ever in vain,
Die one by one in the waste.
Then, in such hour of need
Of your fainting, dispirited race,
Ye, like angels, appear, 190
Radiant with ardour divine!
Beacons of hope, ye appear!
Languour is not in your heart,
Weakness is not in your word,
Weariness not on your brow.
Ye alight in our van! at your voice,
Panic, despair, flee away.

Ye move through the ranks, recall
The stragglers, refresh the outworn,
Praise, re-inspire the brave! 200
Order, courage, return.
Eyes rekindling, and prayers,
Follow your steps as ye go.
Ye fill up the gaps in our files,
Strengthen the wavering line,
Stablish, continue our march,
On, to the bound of the waste,
On, to the City of God.

1867. *Matthew Arnold.*

JOSEPH RODMAN DRAKE

DIED IN NEW YORK, SEPTEMBER, 1820

GREEN be the turf above thee,
Friend of my better days!
None knew thee but to love thee,
Nor named thee but to praise. 4

Tears fell, when thou wert dying,
From eyes unused to weep,
And long, where thou art lying,
Will tears the cold turf steep. 8

When hearts, whose truth was proven,
Like thine, are laid in earth,
There should a wreath be woven
To tell the world their worth; 12

And I, who woke each morrow
  To clasp thy hand in mine,
Who shared thy joy and sorrow,
  Whose weal and woe were thine. 16

It should be mine to braid it
  Around thy faded brow,
But I 've in vain essayed it,
  And feel I cannot now. 20

While memory bids me weep thee,
  Nor thoughts nor words are free,
The grief is fixed too deeply
  That mourns a man like thee. 24

1820. *Fitz-Greene Halleck.*

O CAPTAIN! MY CAPTAIN!

O Captain! my Captain! our fearful trip is done;
The ship has weather'd every rack, the prize we
    sought is won,
The port is near, the bells I hear, the people all
    exulting,
While follow eyes the steady keel, the vessel grim
    and daring:
  But O heart! heart! heart!
    O the bleeding drops of red!
      Where on the deck my Captain lies,
        Fallen cold and dead. 8

O Captain! my Captain! rise up and hear the
bells;
Rise up—for you the flag is flung—for you the
bugle trills;
For you bouquets and ribbon'd wreaths—for you
the shores a-crowding;
For you they call, the swaying mass, their eager
faces turning;
Here, Captain! dear father!
This arm beneath your head!
It is some dream that on the deck,
You've fallen cold and dead. 16

My Captain does not answer, his lips are pale
and still;
My father does not feel my arm, he has no pulse
nor will;
The ship is anchor'd safe and sound, its voyage
closed and done;
From fearful trip the victor ship comes in with
object won:
Exult, O shores! and ring, O bells!
But I, with mournful tread,
Walk the deck my Captain lies,
Fallen cold and dead. 24

1865. *Walt. Whitman.*

ABRAHAM LINCOLN

YOU lay a wreath on murdered Lincoln's bier,
You, who with mocking pencil wont to trace,
Broad for the self-complacent British sneer,
His length of shambling limb, his furrowed face, 4

His gaunt, gnarled hands, his unkempt, bristling hair,
His garb uncouth, his bearing ill at ease,
His lack of all we prize as debonair,
Of power or will to shine, of art to please; 8

You, whose smart pen backed up the pencil's laugh,
Judging each step as though the way were plain,
Reckless, so it could point its paragraph,
Of chief's perplexity, or people's pain,— 12

Beside this corpse, that bears for winding-sheet
The Stars and Stripes he lived to rear anew,
Between the mourners at his head and feet,
Say, scurrile jester, is there room for *you?* 16

Yes: he had lived to shame me from my sneer,
To lame my pencil and confute my pen;
To make me own this hind of princes peer,
This rail-splitter a true-born king of men. 20

My shallow judgment I had learned to rue,
Noting how to occasion's height he rose;
How his quaint wit made home-truth seem more true;
How, iron-like, his temper grew by blows; 24

How humble, yet how hopeful he could be;
How, in good fortune and in ill, the same;
Nor bitter in success, nor boastful he,
Thirsty for gold, nor feverish for fame. 28

He went about his work,—such work as few
Ever had laid on head and heart and hand,—
As one who knows, where there 's a task to do,
Man's honest will must Heaven's good grace command; 32

Who trusts the strength will with the burden grow,
That God makes instruments to work his will,
If but that will we can arrive to know,
Nor tamper with the weights of good and ill. 36

So he went forth to battle, on the side
That he felt clear was Liberty's and Right's,

As in his peasant boyhood he had plied
His warfare with rude Nature's thwarting mights,— 40

The uncleared forest, the unbroken soil,
The iron bark, that turns the lumberer's axe,
The rapid that o'erbears the boatman's toil,
The prairie hiding the mazed wanderer's tracks, 44

The ambushed Indian, and the prowling bear,—
Such were the deeds that helped his youth to train:
Rough culture, but such trees large fruit may bear,
If but their stocks be of right girth and grain. 48

So he grew up, a destined work to do,
And lived to do it; four long-suffering years'
Ill-fate, ill-feeling, ill-report lived through,
And then he heard the hisses changed to cheers, 52

The taunts to tribute, the abuse to praise,
And took both with the same unwavering mood,—
Till, as he came on light from darkling days,
And seemed to touch the goal from where he stood, 56

A felon hand, between the goal and him,
Reached from behind his back, a trigger prest,
And those perplexed and patient eyes were dim,
Those gaunt, long-laboring limbs were laid to rest. 60

The words of mercy were upon his lips,
Forgiveness in his heart and on his pen,
When this vile murderer brought swift eclipse
To thoughts of peace on earth, good-will to men. 64

The Old World and the New, from sea to sea,
Utter one voice of sympathy and shame.
Sore heart, so stopped when it at last beat high!
Sad life, cut short just as its triumph came! 68

A deed accurst! Strokes have been struck before
By the assassin's hand, whereof men doubt
If more of horror or disgrace they bore;
But thy foul crime, like Cain's, stands darkly out, 72

Vile hand, that brandest murder on a strife,
Whate'er its grounds, stoutly and nobly striven;
And with the martyr's crown crownest a life
With much to praise, little to be forgiven. 76

1865. *Tom Taylor.*

CHARLES SUMNER

GARLANDS upon his grave,
And flowers upon his hearse,
And to the tender heart and brave
The tribute of this verse. 4

His was the troubled life,
The conflict and the pain,
The grief, the bitterness of strife,
The honor without stain. 8

Like Winkelried, he took
Into his manly breast
The sheaf of hostile spears, and broke
A path for the oppressed. 12

Then from the fatal field
Upon a nation's heart
Borne like a warrior on his shield!—
So should the brave depart. 16

Death takes us by surprise,
And stays our hurrying feet;
The great design unfinished lies,
Our lives are incomplete. 20

But in the dark unknown
Perfect their circles seem,
Even as a bridge's arch of stone
Is rounded in the stream. 24

Alike are life and death,
When life in death survives,
And the uninterrupted breath
Inspires a thousand lives. 28

Were a star quenched on high,
For ages would its light,
Still travelling downward from the sky,
Shine on our mortal sight. 32

So when a great man dies,
For years beyond our ken,
The light he leaves behind him lies
Upon the paths of men. 36

1874. *Henry Wadsworth Longfellow.*

DIRGE IN CYMBELINE

To fair Fidele's grassy tomb
Soft maids and village hinds shall bring
Each opening sweet of earliest bloom,
And rifle all the breathing Spring. 4

No wailing ghost shall dare appear
To vex with shrieks this quiet grove;

But shepherd lads assemble here,
And melting virgins own their love. 8

No wither'd witch shall here be seen;
No goblins lead their nightly crew:
The female fays shall haunt the green,
And dress thy grave with pearly dew. 12

The redbreast oft at evening hours
Shall kindly lend his little aid,
With hoary moss, and gather'd flowers,
To deck the ground where thou art laid. 16

When howling winds and beating rain,
In tempests shake the sylvan cell;
Or 'midst the chase, on every plain,
The tender thought on thee shall dwell; 20

Each lonely scene shall thee restore;
For thee the tear be duly shed;
Beloved, till life can charm no more;
And mourned, till Pity's self be dead. 24

1749. *William Collins.*

OH! SNATCH'D AWAY IN BEAUTY'S BLOOM

Oh! snatch'd away in beauty's bloom,
On thee shall press no ponderous tomb;
But on thy turf shall roses rear
Their leaves, the earliest of the year;
And the wild cypress wave in tender gloom: 5

And oft by yon blue gushing stream
Shall Sorrow lean her drooping head,
And feed deep thought with many a dream,
And lingering pause and lightly tread;
Fond wretch! as if her step disturb'd the
  dead! 10

Away! we know that tears are vain,
That Death nor heeds nor hears distress:
Will this unteach us to complain?
Or make one mourner weep the less?
And thou, who tell'st me to forget,
Thy looks are wan, thine eyes are wet. 15

1815. *Lord Byron.*

LUCY

I

STRANGE fits of passion have I known:
  And I will dare to tell,
But in the Lover's ear alone,
  What once to me befell. 4

When she I loved look'd every day
  Fresh as a rose in June,
I to her cottage bent my way,
  Beneath an evening-moon. 8

Upon the moon I fix'd my eye,
  All over the wide lea;

With quickening pace my horse drew nigh
  Those paths so dear to me. 12

And now we reach'd the orchard-plot;
  And, as we climb'd the hill,
The sinking moon to Lucy's cot
  Came near, and nearer still. 16

In one of those sweet dreams I slept,
  Kind Nature's gentlest boon!
And all the while my eyes I kept
  On the descending moon. 20

My horse moved on; hoof after hoof
  He raised, and never stopp'd:
When down behind the cottage roof,
  At once, the bright moon dropp'd. 24

What fond and wayward thoughts will slide
  Into a Lover's head!
"O mercy!" to myself I cried,
  "If Lucy should be dead!" 28

1799. 1800.

II

SHE dwelt among the untrodden ways
  Beside the springs of Dove,
A Maid whom there were none to praise
  And very few to love: 4

A violet by a mossy stone
  Half hidden from the eye!

—Fair as a star, when only one
  Is shining in the sky. 8

She lived unknown, and few could know
  When Lucy ceased to be;
But she is in her grave, and oh,
  The difference to me! 12

1799. 1800.

III

I TRAVELL'D among unknown men,
  In lands beyond the sea;
Nor, England! did I know till then
  What love I bore to thee. 4

'T is past, that melancholy dream!
  Nor will I quit thy shore
A second time; for still I seem
  To love thee more and more. 8

Among thy mountains did I feel
  The joy of my desire;
And she I cherish'd turn'd her wheel
  Beside an English fire. 12

Thy mornings show'd, thy nights conceal'd
  The bowers where Lucy play'd;
And thine too is the last green field
  That Lucy's eyes survey'd. 16

1799. 1807.

IV

THREE years she grew in sun and shower;
Then Nature said, "A lovelier flower
  On earth was never sown;
This Child I to myself will take;
She shall be mine, and I will make
  A Lady of my own. 6

"Myself will to my darling be
Both law and impulse: and with me
  The Girl, in rock and plain,
In earth and heaven, in glade and bower,
Shall feel an overseeing power
  To kindle or restrain. 12

"She shall be sportive as the fawn
That wild with glee across the lawn,
  Or up the mountain springs;
And hers shall be the breathing balm,
And hers the silence and the calm
  Of mute insensate things. 18

"The floating clouds their state shall lend
To her; for her the willow bend;
  Nor shall she fail to see
Even in the motions of the Storm
Grace that shall mould the Maiden's form
  By silent sympathy. 24

"The stars of midnight shall be dear
To her; and she shall lean her ear
In many a secret place
Where rivulets dance their wayward round,
And beauty born of murmuring sound
Shall pass into her face. 30

"And vital feelings of delight
Shall rear her form to stately height,
Her virgin bosom swell;
Such thoughts to Lucy I will give
While she and I together live
Here in this happy dell." 36

Thus Nature spake—The work was done—
How soon my Lucy's race was run!
She died, and left to me
This heath, this calm and quiet scene;
The memory of what has been,
And never more will be. 42

1799. 1800.

V

A SLUMBER did my spirit seal;
I had no human fears:
She seem'd a thing that could not feel
The touch of earthly years. 4

No motion has she now, no force;
She neither hears nor sees;
Roll'd round in earth's diurnal course,
With rocks, and stones, and trees. 8

1799. 1800. *William Wordsworth.*

ROSE AYLMER

Ah what avails the sceptred race,
  Ah what the form divine!
What every virtue, every grace!
  Rose Aylmer, all were thine.

Rose Aylmer, whom these wakeful eyes
  May weep, but never see,
A night of memories and of sighs
  I consecrate to thee.

1806. *Walter Savage Landor.*

THE MAID'S LAMENT

I loved him not; and yet, now he is gone,
  I feel I am alone.
I checked him while he spoke; yet could he
    speak,
  Alas! I would not check.
For reasons not to love him once I sought,
  And wearied all my thought
To vex myself and him: I now would give
  My love, could he but live
Who lately lived for me, and when he found
  'T was vain, in holy ground 10

He hid his face amid the shades of death.
  I waste for him my breath
Who wasted his for me; but mine returns,
  And this lorn bosom burns
With stifling heat, heaving it up in sleep,
  And waking me to weep
Tears that had melted his soft heart: for years
  Wept he as bitter tears.
"Merciful God!" such was his latest prayer,
  "These may she never share!"
Quieter is his breath, his breast more cold
  Than daisies in the mould,
Where children spell, athwart the churchyard
    gate,
  His name and life's brief date.
Pray for him, gentle souls, whoe'er ye be,
  And O! pray too for me!

1834. ***Walter Savage Landor.***

REQUIESCAT

STREW on her roses, roses,
  And never a spray of yew!
In quiet she reposes;
  Ah, would that I did too! 4

Her mirth the world required;
  She bathed it in smiles of glee.
But her heart was tired, tired,
  And now they let her be. 8

Her life was turning, turning,
  In mazes of heat and sound.
But for peace her soul was yearning,
  And now peace laps her round. 12

Her cabin'd, ample spirit,
  It flutter'd and fail'd for breath.
To-night it doth inherit
  The vasty hall of death. 16

1853. *Matthew Arnold.*

EVELYN HOPE

Beautiful Evelyn Hope is dead!
  Sit and watch by her side an hour.
That is her book-shelf, this her bed;
  She plucked that piece of geranium-flower,
Beginning to die too, in the glass;
  Little has yet been changed, I think:
The shutters are shut, no light may pass
  Save two long rays through the hinge's
    chink. 8

Sixteen years old when she died!
  Perhaps she had scarcely heard my name;
It was not her time to love; beside,
  Her life had many a hope and aim,
Duties enough and little cares,
  And now was quiet, now astir,
Till God's hand beckoned unawares,—
  And the sweet white brow is all of her. 16

Is it too late then, Evelyn Hope?
  What, your soul was pure and true,
The good stars met in your horoscope,
  Made you of spirit, fire and dew—
And, just because I was thrice as old
  And our paths in the world diverged so wide,
Each was naught to each, must I be told?
  We were fellow mortals, naught beside? 24

No, indeed! for God above
  Is great to grant, as mighty to make,
And creates the love to reward the love:
  I claim you still, for my own love's sake!
Delayed it may be for more lives yet,
  Through worlds I shall traverse, not a few:
Much is to learn, much to forget
  Ere the time be come for taking you. 32

But the time will come,—at last it will,
  When, Evelyn Hope, what meant (I shall say)
In the lower earth, in the years long still,
  That body and soul so pure and gay?
Why your hair was amber, I shall divine,
  And your mouth of your own geranium's red—
And what you would do with me, in fine,
  In the new life come in the old life's stead. 40

I have lived (I shall say) so much since then,
  Given up myself so many times,

Gained me the gains of various men,
  Ransacked the ages, spoiled the climes;
Yet one thing, one, in my soul's full scope,
  Either I missed or itself missed me:
And I want and find you, Evelyn Hope!
  What is the issue? Let us see! 48

I loved you, Evelyn, all the while!
  My heart seemed full as it could hold;
There was place and to spare for the frank
    young smile,
  And the red young mouth, and the hair's
    young gold.
So, hush,—I will give you this leaf to keep:
  See, I shut it inside the sweet cold hand!
There, that is our secret: go to sleep!
  You will wake, and remember, and under-
    stand. 56

1855. *Robert Browning.*

MAY AND DEATH

I WISH that when you died last May,
  Charles, there had died along with you
Three parts of Spring's delightful things;
  Ay, and, for me, the fourth part too. 4

A foolish thought, and worse, perhaps!
  There must be many a pair of friends
Who, arm in arm, deserve the warm
  Moon-births and the long evening-ends. 8

So, for their sake, be May still May!
  Let their new time, as mine of old,
Do all it did for me: I bid
  Sweet sights and sounds throng manifold. 12

Only, one little sight, one plant,
  Woods have in May, that starts up green
Save a sole streak which, so to speak,
  Is Spring's blood, spilt its leaves
    between,— 16

That, they might spare; a certain wood
  Might miss the plant; their loss were small:
But I,—whene'er the leaf grows there,
  Its drop comes from my heart, that 's all. 20

1857. *Robert Browning.*

THE BRIDGE OF SIGHS

"Drowned! drowned!"—HAMLET

ONE more Unfortunate,
Weary of breath,
Rashly importunate,
Gone to her death! 4

Take her up tenderly,
Lift her with care;
Fashioned so slenderly,
Young, and so fair! 8

The Bridge of Sighs

Look at her garments
Clinging like cerements,
Whilst the wave constantly
Drips from her clothing;
Take her up instantly,
Loving, not loathing.— 14

Touch her not scornfully;
Think of her mournfully,
Gently and humanly;
Not of the stains of her,
All that remains of her,
Now is pure womanly. 20

Make no deep scrutiny
Into her mutiny,
Rash and undutiful;
Past all dishonor,
Death has left on her
Only the beautiful. 26

Still, for all slips of hers,—
One of Eve's family,—
Wipe those poor lips of hers,
Oozing so clammily. 30

Loop up her tresses
Escaped from the comb,—
Her fair auburn tresses,—
Whilst wonderment guesses
Where was her home? 35

Who was her father?
Who was her mother?
Had she a sister?
Had she a brother?
Or was there a dearer one
Still, and a nearer one
Yet, than all other? 42

Alas! for the rarity
Of Christian charity
Under the sun!
Oh! it was pitiful!
Near a whole city full,
Home she had none. 48

Sisterly, brotherly,
Fatherly, motherly
Feelings had changed,—
Love, by harsh evidence,
Thrown from its eminence;
Even God's providence
Seeming estranged. 55

Where the lamps quiver
So far in the river,
With many a light
From window and casement,
From garret to basement,
She stood, with amazement,
Houseless by night. 62

The Bridge of Sighs

The bleak wind of March
Made her tremble and shiver;
But not the dark arch,
Or the black flowing river;
Mad from life's history,
Glad to death's mystery,
Swift to be hurled—
Anywhere, anywhere
Out of the world! 71

In she plunged boldly,—
No matter how coldly
The rough river ran,—
Over the brink of it,
Picture it—think of it,
Dissolute Man!
Lave in it, drink of it,
Then, if you can! 79

Take her up tenderly,
Lift her with care;
Fashioned so slenderly,
Young, and so fair! 83

Ere her limbs, frigidly,
Stiffen too rigidly,
Decently, kindly,
Smooth and compose them;
And her eyes, close them,
Staring so blindly! 89

Dreadfully staring
Through muddy impurity,
As when with the daring
Last look of despairing
Fixed on futurity. 94

Perishing gloomily,
Spurred by contumely,
Cold inhumanity,
Burning insanity,
Into her rest.—
Cross her hands humbly,
As if praying dumbly,
Over her breast! 102

Owning her weakness,
Her evil behavior,
And leaving, with meekness,
Her sins to her Saviour! 106

1844. *Thomas Hood.*

LAMENT OF THE IRISH EMIGRANT

I 'M sittin' on the stile, Mary,
  Where we sat side by side
On a bright May mornin' long ago,
  When first you were my bride;
The corn was springin' fresh and green,
  And the lark sang loud and high—
And the red was on your lip, Mary,
  And the love-light in your eye. 8

Lament of the Irish Emigrant

The *place* is little changed, Mary,
The day is bright as then,
The lark's loud song is in my ear,
And the corn is green again;
But I miss the soft clasp of your hand,
And your breath warm on my cheek,
And I still keep list'ning for the words
You never more will speak. 16

'T is but a step down yonder lane,
And the little church stands near,
The church where we were wed, Mary,
I see the spire from here.
But the graveyard lies between, Mary,
And my step might break your rest—
For I 've laid you, darling! down to sleep,
With your baby on your breast. 24

I 'm very lonely now, Mary,
For the poor make no new friends,
But, oh! they love the better still,
The few our Father sends!
And you were all *I* had, Mary,
My blessin' and my pride:
There 's nothin' left to care for now,
Since my poor Mary died. 32

Yours was the good, brave heart, Mary,
That still kept hoping on,
When the trust in God had left my soul,
And my arm's young strength was gone:

There was comfort ever on your lip,
  And the kind look on your brow—
I bless you, Mary, for that same,
  Though you cannot hear me now. 40

I thank you for the patient smile
  When your heart was fit to break,
When the hunger pain was gnawin' there,
  And you hid it, for *my* sake!
I bless you for the pleasant word,
  When your heart was sad and sore—
Oh! I 'm thankful you are gone, Mary,
  Where grief can't reach you more! 48

I 'm biddin' you a long farewell,
  My Mary—kind and true!
But I 'll not forget you, darling!
  In the land I 'm goin' to;
They say there 's bread and work for all.
  And the sun shines always there—
But I 'll not forget old Ireland,
  Were it fifty times as fair! 56

And often in those grand old woods
  I 'll sit, and shut my eyes,
And my heart will travel back again
  To the place where Mary lies;
And I 'll think I see the little stile
  Where we sat side by side:
And the springin' corn, and the bright May
    morn,
  When first you were my bride. 64

1845. *Helen Selina, Lady Dufferin.*

THE DEATH BED

We watch'd her breathing thro' the night,
  Her breathing soft and low,
As in her breast the wave of life
  Kept heaving to and fro. 4

So silently we seem'd to speak,
  So slowly moved about,
As we had lent her half our powers
  To eke her living out. 8

Our very hopes belied our fears,
  Our fears our hopes belied—
We thought her dying when she slept,
  And sleeping when she died. 12

For when the morn came dim and sad
  And chill with early showers,
Her quiet eyelids closed—she had
  Another morn than ours. 16

1831. *Thomas Hood.*

RESIGNATION

There is no flock, however watched and tended,
  But one dead lamb is there!
There is no fireside, howsoe'er defended,
  But has one vacant chair! 4

The air is full of farewells to the dying,
  And mournings for the dead;
The heart of Rachel, for her children crying,
  Will not be comforted! 8

Let us be patient! These severe afflictions
  Not from the ground arise,
But oftentimes celestial benedictions
  Assume this dark disguise. 12

We see but dimly through the mists and vapors;
  Amid these earthly damps
What seem to us but sad, funeral tapers
  May be heaven's distant lamps. 16

There is no Death! What seems so is transi-
    tion;
  This life of mortal breath
Is but a suburb of the life elysian,
  Whose portal we call Death. 20

She is not dead,—the child of our affection,—
  But gone unto that school
Where she no longer needs our poor protection,
  And Christ himself doth rule. 24

In that great cloister's stillness and seclusion,
  By guardian angels led,
Safe from temptation, safe from sin's pollution,
  She lives, whom we call dead. 28

Resignation

Day after day we think what she is doing
  In those bright realms of air;
Year after year, her tender steps pursuing,
  Behold her grown more fair. 32

Thus do we walk with her, and keep unbroken
  The bond which nature gives,
Thinking that our remembrance, though unspoken,
  May reach her where she lives. 36

Not as a child shall we again behold her;
  For when with raptures wild
In our embraces we again enfold her,
  She will not be a child; 40

But a fair maiden, in her Father's mansion,
  Clothed with celestial grace;
And beautiful with all the soul's expansion
  Shall we behold her face. 44

And though at times impetuous with emotion
  And anguish long suppressed,
The swelling heart heaves moaning like the ocean,
  That cannot be at rest,— 48

We will be patient, and assuage the feeling
  We may not wholly stay;
By silence sanctifying, not concealing,
  The grief that must have way. 52

1849. *Henry Wadsworth Longfellow.*

SHE CAME AND WENT

As a twig trembles, which a bird
  Lights on to sing, then leaves unbent,
So is my memory thrilled and stirred;—
  I only know she came and went. 4

As clasps some lake, by gusts unriven,
  The blue dome's measureless content,
So my soul held that moment's heaven;—
  I only know she came and went. 8

As, at one bound, our swift spring heaps
  The orchards full of bloom and scent,
So clove her May my wintry sleeps;—
  I only know she came and went. 12

An angel stood and met my gaze,
  Through the low doorway of my tent;
The tent is struck, the vision stays;—
  I only know she came and went. 16

Oh, when the room grows slowly dim,
  And life's last oil is nearly spent,
One gush of light these eyes will brim,
  Only to think she came and went. 20

1849. *James Russell Lowell.*

THE FIRST SNOW-FALL

THE snow had begun in the gloaming,
  And busily all the night
Had been heaping field and highway
  With a silence deep and white. 4

Every pine and fir and hemlock
  Wore ermine too dear for an earl,
And the poorest twig on the elm-tree
  Was ridged inch deep with pearl. 8

From sheds new-roofed with Carrara
  Came Chanticleer's muffled crow,
The stiff rails softened to swan's-down,
  And still fluttered down the snow. 12

I stood and watched by the window
  The noiseless work of the sky,
And the sudden flurries of snow-birds,
  Like brown leaves whirling by. 16

I thought of a mound in sweet Auburn
  Where a little headstone stood;
How the flakes were folding it gently,
  As did robins the babes in the wood. 20

Up spoke our own little Mabel
  Saying, "Father, who makes it snow?"
And I told of the good All-father
  Who cares for us here below. 24

Again I looked at the snow-fall,
  And thought of the leaden sky
That arched o'er our first great sorrow,
  When that mound was heaped so high. 28

I remembered the gradual patience
  That fell from that cloud like snow,
Flake by flake, healing and hiding
  The scar that renewed our woe. 32

And again to the child I whispered,
  "The snow that husheth all,
Darling, the merciful Father
  Alone can make it fall!" 36

Then, with eyes that saw not, I kissed her;
  And she, kissing back, could not know
That *my* kiss was given to her sister,
  Folded close under deepening snow. 40

1849. *James Russell Lowell.*

A DEATH-BED

Her suffering ended with the day,
  Yet lived she at its close,
And breathed the long, long night away
  In a statue-like repose. 4

But when the sun in all his state
  Illumed the eastern skies,
She passed through Glory's morning gate
  And walked in Paradise! 8

c. *1840.* *James Aldrich.*

MY SISTER'S SLEEP

She fell asleep on Christmas Eve:
  At length the long-ungranted shade
  Of weary eyelids overweigh'd
The pain nought else might yet relieve. 4

Our mother, who had leaned all day
  Over the bed from chime to chime,
  Then raised herself for the first time,
And as she sat her down, did pray. 8

Her little work-table was spread
  With work to finish. For the glare
  Made by her candle, she had care
To work some distance from the bed. 12

Without, there was a cold moon up,
  Of winter radiance sheer and thin;
  The hollow halo it was in
Was like an icy crystal cup. 16

Through the small room, with subtle sound
Of flame, by vents the fireshine drove
And reddened. In its dim alcove
The mirror shed a clearness round. 20

I had been sitting up some nights,
And my tired mind felt weak and blank;
Like a sharp strengthening wine it drank
The stillness and the broken lights. 24

Twelve struck. That sound, by dwindling years
Heard in each hour, crept off; and then
The ruffled silence spread again,
Like water that a pebble stirs. 28

Our mother rose from where she sat:
Her needles, as she laid them down,
Met lightly, and her silken gown
Settled: no other noise than that. 32

"Glory unto the Newly Born!"
So, as said angels, she did say;
Because we were in Christmas Day,
Though it would still be long till morn. 36

Just then in the room over us
There was a pushing back of chairs,
As some who had sat unawares
So late, now heard the hour, and rose. 40

With anxious softly-stepping haste
  Our mother went where Margaret lay,
  Fearing the sounds o'erhead—should they
Have broken her long watched-for rest! 44

She stooped an instant, calm, and turned;
  But suddenly turned back again;
  And all her features seemed in pain
With woe, and her eyes gazed and yearned. 48

For my part, I but hid my face,
  And held my breath, and spoke no word:
  There was none spoken; but I heard
The silence for a little space. 52

Our mother bowed herself and wept:
  And both my arms fell, and I said,
  "God knows I knew that she was dead."
And there, all white, my sister slept. 56

Then kneeling, upon Christmas morn
  A little after twelve o'clock,
  We said, ere the first quarter struck,
"Christ's blessing on the newly born!" 60

1847. 1850. *Dante Gabriel Rossetti.*

THE MOTHER'S DREAM

I 'D a dream to-night
  As I fell asleep,
Oh! the touching sight
  Makes me still to weep:

Of my little lad,
Gone to leave me sad,
Aye, the child I had,
  But was not to keep. 8

As in heaven high,
  I my child did seek,
There, in train, came by
  Children fair and meek,
Each in lily-white,
With a lamp alight;
Each was clear to sight,
  But they did not speak. 16

Then, a little sad,
  Came my child in turn,
But the lamp he had,
  Oh! it did not burn;
He, to clear my doubt,
Said, half turn'd about,
"Your tears put it out;
  Mother, never mourn." 24

1868. *William Barnes.*

THE TOYS

My little Son, who look'd from thoughtful eyes
And moved and spoke in quiet grown-up wise,
Having my law the seventh time disobey'd,
I struck him, and dismiss'd
With hard words and unkiss'd,

—His Mother, who was patient, being dead.
Then, fearing lest his grief should hinder sleep,
I visited his bed,
But found him slumbering deep,
With darken'd eyelids, and their lashes yet   10
From his late sobbing wet.
And I, with moan,
Kissing away his tears, left others of my own;
For, on a table drawn beside his head,
He had put, within his reach,
A box of counters and a red-vein'd stone,
A piece of glass abraded by the beach,
And six or seven shells,
A bottle with bluebells,
And two French copper coins, ranged there
with careful art,   20
To comfort his sad heart.
So when that night I pray'd
To God, I wept, and said:
Ah, when at last we lie with trancèd breath,
Not vexing Thee in death,
And Thou rememberest of what toys
We made our joys,
How weakly understood,
Thy great commanded good,
Then, fatherly not less   30
Than I whom Thou hast moulded from the clay,
Thou'lt leave Thy wrath, and say,
"I will be sorry for their childishness."

1877. *Coventry Patmore.*

REQUIEM

UNDER the wide and starry sky,
  Dig the grave and let me lie.
Glad did I live and gladly die,
  And I laid me down with a will.

This be the verse you grave for me:
Here he lies where he long'd to be;
Home is the sailor, home from sea,
  And the hunter home from the hill.

1884. 1887. *Robert Louis Stevenson.*

IN HARBOR[1]

I THINK it is over, over,
  I think it is over at last:
Voices of foeman and lover,
  The sweet and the bitter have passed:
Life, like a tempest of ocean
  Hath outblown its ultimate blast:
There 's but a faint sobbing seaward
While the calm of the tide deepens leeward,
And behold! like the welcoming quiver
Of heart-pulses throbbed through the river,
  Those lights in the harbor at last,
  The heavenly harbor at last! 12

Epilogue

I feel it is over! over!
  For the winds and the waters surcease;
Ah, few were the days of the rover
  That smiled in the beauty of peace,
And distant and dim was the omen
That hinted redress or release!
From the ravage of life, and its riot,
What marvel I yearn for the quiet
  Which bides in the harbor at last,—
For the lights, with their welcoming quiver
That throbs through the sanctified river,
  Which girdle the harbor at last,
  This heavenly harbor at last? 24

I know it is over, over
  I know it is over at last!
Down sail! the sheathed anchor uncover,
For the stress of the voyage has passed:
Life, like a tempest of ocean,
  Hath outbreathed its ultimate blast:
There 's but a faint sobbing seaward,
While the calm of the tide deepens leeward;
And behold! like the welcoming quiver
Of heart-pulses throbbed through the river,
  Those lights in the harbor at last,
  The heavenly harbor at last! 36

1882. *Paul Hamilton Hayne.*

EPILOGUE

At the midnight in the silence of the sleep-time,
  When you set your fancies free,

Will they pass to where—by death, fools think,
 Imprisoned—
Low he lies who once so loved you, whom you
 loved so,
 —Pity me? 5

Oh to love so, be so loved, yet so mistaken!
 What had I on earth to do
With the slothful, with the mawkish, the
 unmanly?
Like the aimless, helpless, hopeless, did I drivel
 —Being—who? 10

One who never turned his back but marched
 breast forward,
 Never doubted clouds would break,
Never dreamed, though right were worsted,
 wrong would triumph,
Held we fall to rise, are baffled to fight better,
 Sleep to wake. 15

No, at noonday in the bustle of man's work-time
 Greet the unseen with a cheer!
Bid him forward, breast and back as either
 should be,
"Strive and thrive!" cry "Speed,—fight on, fare
 ever
 There as here!" 20

1889. *Robert Browning.*

PROSPICE

Fear death?—to feel the fog in my throat,
  The mist in my face,
When the snows begin, and the blasts denote
  I am nearing the place,
The power of the night, the press of the storm,
  The post of the foe;
Where he stands, the Arch Fear in a visible
    form,
  Yet the strong man must go:
For the journey is done and the summit
    attained,
  And the barriers fall, 10
Though a battle 's to fight ere the guerdon be
    gained,
  The reward of it all.
I was ever a fighter, so—one fight more,
  The best and the last!
I would hate that death bandaged my eyes, and
    forebore,
  And bade me creep past.
No! let me taste the whole of it, fare like my
    peers
  The heroes of old,
Bear the brunt, in a minute pay glad life's
    arrears
  Of pain, darkness and cold. 20

For sudden the worst turns the best to the
brave,
The black minute's at end,
And the elements' rage, the fiend-voices that
rave,
Shall dwindle, shall blend,
Shall change, shall become first a peace out of
pain,
Then a light, then thy breast,
O thou soul of my soul! I shall clasp thee
again,
And with God be the rest!

1861. 1864. *Robert Browning.*

HYMNS AND POEMS OF FAITH

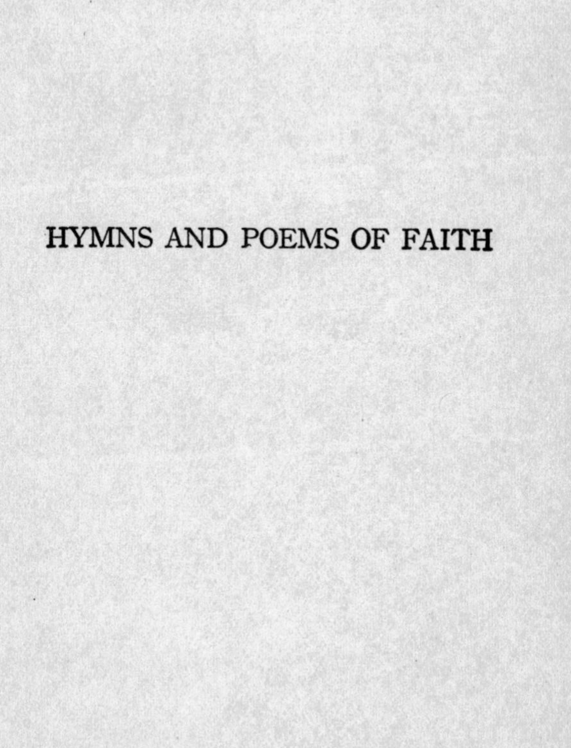

A CHILD MY CHOICE

LET folly praise that fancy loves, I praise and love
 that Child
Whose heart no thought, whose tongue no word,
 whose hand no deed defiled.
I praise Him most, I love Him best, all praise and
 love is His;
While Him I love, in Him I live, and cannot live
 amiss.
Love's sweetest mark, laud's highest theme,
 man's most desired light,
To love Him life, to leave Him death, to live in
 Him delight.
He mine by gift, I His by debt, thus each to other
 due,
First friend He was, best friend He is, all times
 will try Him true.
Though young, yet wise, though small, yet strong;
 though man, yet God He is; 9
As wise He knows, as strong He can, as God He
 loves to bliss.
His knowledge rules, His strength defends, His
 love doth cherish all;
His birth our joy, His life our light, His death
 our end of thrall.

Alas! He weeps, He sighs, He pants, yet do His angels sing;
Out of His tears, His sighs and throbs, doth bud a joyful spring.
Almighty Babe, whose tender arms can force all foes to fly,
Correct my faults, protect my life, direct me when I die! 16

Robert Southwell.

THE ELIXIR

Teach me, my God and King,
In all things Thee to see,
And what I do in anything,
To do it as for Thee. 4

Not rudely, as a beast,
To run into an action;
But still to make Thee prepossesst,
And give it his perfection. 8

A man that looks on glass,
On it may stay his eye;
Or if he pleaseth, through it pass,
And then the Heav'n espy. 12

All may of Thee partake:
Nothing can be so mean
Which with his tincture, for Thy sake,
Will not grow bright and clean. 16

A servant with this clause
  Makes drudgery divine;
Who sweeps a room as for Thy laws
  Makes that and th' action fine. 20

This is the famous stone
  That turneth all to gold;
For that which God doth touch and own
  Cannot for less be told. 24

1633. *George Herbert.*

DISCIPLINE

Throw away Thy rod,
Throw away Thy wrath;
    O my God,
Take the gentle path. 4

For my heart's desire
Unto Thine is bent;
    I aspire
To a full consent. 8

Not a word or look
I affect to own,
    But by book,
And Thy Book alone. 12

Though I fail, I weep;
Though I halt in pace,
    Yet I creep
To the throne of grace. 16

Then let wrath remove;
Love will do the deed;
  For with love
Stony hearts will bleed. 16

Love is swift of foot;
Love 's a man of war,
  And can shoot,
And can hit from far. 24

Who can 'scape his bow?
That which wrought on Thee,
  Brought Thee low,
Needs must work on me. 28

Throw away Thy rod:
Though man frailties hath,
  Thou art God;
Throw away Thy wrath. 32

1633. *George Herbert.*

EASTER

I GOT me flowers to straw Thy way,
  I got me boughs off many a tree;
But Thou wast up by break of day,
  And brought'st Thy sweets along with
    Thee. 4

The sun arising in the East,
  Though he give light, and th' East
    perfume,

If they should offer to contest
With Thy arising, they presume. 8

Yet though my flowers be lost, they say
A heart can never come too late;
Teach it to sing Thy praise this day,
And then this day my life shall date. 12

1633. *George Herbert.*

THE PULLEY

When God at first made Man,
Having a glass of blessings standing by—
Let us (said He) pour on him all we can;
Let the world's riches, which dispersèd lie,
Contract into a span. 5

So strength first made a way,
Then beauty flow'd, then wisdom, honour, pleasure;
When almost all was out, God made a stay,
Perceiving that, alone of all His treasure,
Rest in the bottom lay. 10

For if I should (said He)
Bestow this jewel also on My creature,
He would adore My gifts instead of Me,
And rest in Nature, not the God of Nature:
So both should losers be. 15

Yet let him keep the rest,
But keep them with repining restlessness;
Let him be rich and weary, that at least,
If goodness lead him not, yet weariness
May toss him to My breast. 20

1633. *George Herbert.*

VIRTUE

Sweet day, so cool, so calm, so bright!
The bridal of the earth and sky—
The dew shall weep thy fall to-night;
For thou must die. 4

Sweet rose, whose hue angry and brave
Bids the rash gazer wipe his eye,
Thy root is ever in its grave,
And thou must die. 8

Sweet spring, full of sweet days and roses,
A box where sweets compacted lie,
My music shows ye have your closes,
And all must die. 12

Only a sweet and virtuous soul,
Like season'd timber, never gives;
But though the whole world turn to coal,
Then chiefly lives. 16

1633. *George Herbert.*

GEORGE HERBERT

LOVE TRIUMPHANT

E'EN like two little bank-dividing brooks,
That wash the pebbles with their wanton streams,
And having ranged and search'd a thousand nooks,
Meet both at length in silver-breasted Thames,
Where in a greater current they conjoin:
So I my Best-Belovèd's am; so He is mine. 6

E'en so we met; and after long pursuit,
E'en so we join'd: we both became entire;
No need for either to renew a suit,
For I was flax and he was flames of fire:
Our firm-united souls did more than twine;
So I my Best-Belovèd's am; so He is mine. 12

If all those glittering Monarchs that command
The servile quarters of this earthly ball,
Should tender, in exchange, their shares of land,
I would not change my fortunes for them all:
Their wealth is but a counter to my coin:
The world 's but theirs; but my Belovèd 's mine. 18

1635? *Francis Quarles.*

THE WILL

BEFORE I sigh my last gasp, let me breathe,
Great Love, some legacies: here I bequeathe
Mine eyes to Argus, if mine eyes can see;
If they be blind, then, Love, I give them thee;
My tongue to Fame; to embassadors mine ears;
To women or the sea, my tears;
Thou, Love, hast taught me heretofore
By making me serve her who had twenty more,
That I should give to none, but such as had too
much before. 9

My constancy I to the planets give;
My truth to them who at the court do live;
Mine ingenuity and openness,
To Jesuits; to buffoons my pensiveness;
My silence to any, who abroad have been;
My money to a Capuchin:
Thou, Love, taught'st me, by appointing me
To love there, where no love received can be,
Only to give to such as have an incapacity. 18

My faith I give to Roman Catholics;
All my good works unto the schismatics
Of Amsterdam; my best civility
And courtship to an University;

The Will

My modesty I give to shoulders bare;
My patience let gamesters share:
Thou, Love, taught'st me, by making me
Love her that holds my love disparity,
Only to give to those that count my gifts indignity. 27

I give my reputation to those
Which were my friends; mine industry to foes;
To schoolmen I bequeathe my doubtfulness;
My sickness to physicians, or excess;
To Nature all that I in rhyme have writ;
And to my company my wit:
Thou, Love, by making me adore
Her, who begot this love in me before,
Taught'st me to make, as though I gave, when I do but restore. 36

To him, for whom the passing-bell next tolls,
I give my physic-books; my written rolls
Of moral counsels I to Bedlam give;
My brazen medals unto them which live
In want of bread; to them which pass among
All foreigners, mine English tongue:
Thou, Love, by making me love one
Who thinks her friendship a fit portion
For younger lovers, dost my gifts thus disproportion. 45

Therefore I'll give no more, but I'll undo
The world by dying; because Love dies too.

Then all your beauties will be no more worth
Than gold in mines, where none doth draw it
forth;
And all your graces no more use shall have,
Than a sun-dial in a grave:
Thou, Love, taught'st me, by making me
Love her, who doth neglect both me and thee,
To invent and practise this one way to annihilate
all three. 54

1633. *Dr. John Donne.*

LITANY TO THE HOLY SPIRIT

In the hour of my distress,
When temptations me oppress,
And when I my sins confess,
Sweet Spirit, comfort me! 4

When I lie within my bed,
Sick in heart and sick in head,
And with doubts discomforted,
Sweet Spirit, comfort me! 8

When the house doth sigh and weep,
And the world is drown'd in sleep,
Yet mine eyes the watch do keep,
Sweet Spirit, comfort me! 12

When the artless doctor sees
No one hope, but of his fees,
And his skill runs on the lees,
Sweet Spirit, comfort me! 16

When his potion and his pill
Has, or none, or little skill,
Meet for nothing, but to kill;
Sweet Spirit, comfort me! 20

When the passing bell doth toll,
And the Furies in a shoal
Come to fright a parting soul,
Sweet Spirit, comfort me! 24

When the tapers now burn blue,
And the comforters are few,
And that number more than true,
Sweet Spirit, comfort me! 28

When the priest his last hath pray'd,
And I nod to what is said,
'Cause my speech is now decay'd,
Sweet Spirit, comfort me! 32

When, God knows, I 'm toss'd about,
Either with despair or doubt;
Yet before the glass be out,
Sweet Spirit, comfort me! 36

When the tempter me pursu'th
With the sins of all my youth,
And half damns me with untruth,
Sweet Spirit, comfort me! 40

When the flames and hellish cries
Fright mine ears, and fright mine eyes,
And all terrors me surprise,
Sweet Spirit, comfort me! 44

When the Judgment is reveal'd,
And that open'd which was seal'd,
When to Thee I have appeal'd,
Sweet Spirit, comfort me! 48

1647. *Robert Herrick.*

PEACE

My soul, there is a country
Far beyond the stars,
Where stands a wingèd sentry
All skilful in the wars:
There, above noise and danger,
Sweet Peace sits crown'd with smiles,
And One born in a manger
Commands the beauteous files.
He is thy gracious Friend,
And—O my soul, awake!— 10
Did in pure love descend,
To die here for thy sake.
If thou canst get but thither,
There grows the flower of Peace,
The Rose that cannot wither,
Thy fortress, and thy ease.

Leave then thy foolish ranges;
For none can thee secure
But One who never changes—
Thy God, thy life, thy cure. 20

1650 *Henry Vaughan.*

THE RETREAT

HAPPY those early days, when I
Shin'd in my Angel-infancy!
Before I understood this place
Appointed for my second race,
Or taught my soul to fancy aught
But a white, celestial thought;
When yet I had not walk'd above
A mile or two from my first Love,
And looking back, at that short space
Could see a glimpse of his bright face; 10
When on some gilded cloud or flower
My gazing soul would dwell an hour,
And in those weaker glories spy
Some shadows of eternity;
Before I taught my tongue to wound
My conscience with a sinful sound,
Or had the black art to dispense
A several sin to every sense,
But felt through all this fleshly dress
Bright shoots of everlastingness. 20

O how I long to travel back,
And tread again that ancient track!

That I might once more reach that plain,
Where first I left my glorious train;
From whence th' enlighten'd spirit sees
That shady City of Palm-trees!
But ah! my soul with too much stay
Is drunk, and staggers in the way!
Some men a forward motion love,
But I by backward steps would move; 30
And when this dust falls to the urn,
In that state I came, return.

1650. *Henry Vaughan.*

BERMUDAS

Where the remote Bermudas ride,
In the ocean's bosom unespied,
From a small boat that row'd along
The listening winds received this song:
"What should we do but sing His praise
That led us through the watery maze
Unto an isle so long unknown,
And yet far kinder than our own?
Where He the huge sea monsters wracks,
That lift the deep upon their backs; 10
He lands us on a grassy stage,
Safe from the storms, and prelate's rage.
He gave us this eternal spring
Which here enamels everything,
And sends the fowls to us in care
On daily visits through the air;

He hangs in shades the orange bright,
Like golden lamps in a green night,
And does in the pomegranates close
Jewels more rich than Ormus shows: 20
He makes the figs our mouths to meet,
And throws the melons at our feet;
But apples plants of such a price,
No tree could ever bear them twice;
With cedars chosen by His hand
From Lebanon He stores the land;
And makes the hollow seas that roar
Proclaim the ambergris on shore;
He cast (of which we rather boast)
The Gospel's pearl upon our coast; 30
And in these rocks for us did frame
A temple where to sound His name.
Oh! let our voice His praise exalt
Till it arrive at Heaven's vault,
Which thence (perhaps) rebounding, may
Echo beyond the Mexique bay!"
—Thus sung they in the English boat
A holy and a cheerful note;
And all the way, to guide their chime,
With falling oars they kept the time. 40

1681. *Andrew Marvell.*

THE INVITATION

Lord, what unvalued pleasures crown'd
The days of old;
When Thou were so familiar found,
Those days were gold;— 4

When Abram wish'd Thou couldst afford
With him to feast;
When Lot but said, "Turn in, my Lord,"
Thou wert his guest. 8

But, ah! this heart of mine doth pant,
And beat for Thee;
Yet Thou art strange, and wilt not grant
Thyself to me. 12

What, shall Thy people be so dear
To Thee no more?
Or is not heaven to earth as near
As heretofore? 16

The famish'd raven's hoarser cry
Finds out Thine ear;
My soul is famish'd, and I die
Unless Thou hear. 20

O Thou great Alpha! Kings of kings!
Or bow to me,
Or lend my soul seraphic wings,
To get to Thee. 24

Anonymous.

A HYMN OF TRUST

Lord, it belongs not to my care,
Whether I die or live;
To love and serve Thee is my share,
And this Thy grace must give. 4

If life be long I will be glad,
  That I may long obey;
If short—yet why should I be sad
  To soar to endless day? 8

Christ leads me through no darker rooms
  Than he went through before;
He that unto God's kingdom comes,
  Must enter by this door. 12

Come, Lord, when grace has made me meet
  Thy blessèd face to see;
For if Thy work on earth be sweet,
  What will Thy glory be! 16

Then I shall end my sad complaints,
  And weary, sinful days;
And join with the the triumphant saints,
  To sing Jehovah's praise. 20

My knowledge of that life is small,
  The eye of faith is dim;
But 't is enough that Christ knows all,
  And I shall be with Him. 24

1683. *Richard Baxter.*

THE VOICE OF THE HEAVENS

The spacious firmament on high,
With all the blue ethereal sky,
And spangled heavens, a shining frame,
Their great Original proclaim.

Th' unwearied Sun from day to day
Does his Creator's power display;
And publishes, to every land,
The work of an Almighty hand. 8

Soon as the evening shades prevail,
The Moon takes up the wondrous tale;
And nightly, to the listening Earth,
Repeats the story of her birth:
Whilst all the stars that round her burn,
And all the planets in their turn,
Confirm the tidings as they roll,
And spread the truth from pole to pole. 16

What though in solemn silence all
Move round the dark terrestrial ball;
What though nor real voice nor sound
Amidst their radiant orbs be found?
In Reason's ear they all rejoice,
And utter forth a glorious voice;
For ever singing as they shine:
"The Hand that made us is divine." 24

1712. *Joseph Addison.*

THE UNIVERSAL PRAYER

Father of all! in every age,
  In every clime adored,
By saint, by savage, and by sage,
  Jehovah, Jove, or Lord! 4

The Universal Prayer

Thou Great First Cause, least understood,
  Who all my sense confined
To know but this, that thou art good,
  And that myself am blind: 8

Yet gave me, in this dark estate,
  To see the good from ill;
And binding Nature fast in Fate,
  Left free the human Will. 12

What Conscience dictates to be done,
  Or warns me not to do;
This teach me more than Hell to shun,
  That more than Heaven pursue. 16

What blessings thy free bounty gives
  Let me not cast away;
For God is paid when man receives;
  T' enjoy is to obey. 20

Yet not to earth's contracted span
  Thy goodness let me bound,
Or think thee Lord alone of man,
  When thousand worlds are round. 24

Let not this weak unknowing hand
  Presume thy bolts to throw,
And deal damnation round the land
  On each I judge thy foe. 28

If I am right, thy grace impart,
  Still in the right to stay;

If I am wrong, O teach my heart
  To find that better way. 32

Save me alike from foolish Pride
  And impious Discontent,
At aught thy wisdom has denied,
  Or aught thy goodness lent. 36

Teach me to feel another's woe,
  To hide the fault I see:
That mercy I to others show,
  That mercy show to me. 40

Mean though I am, not wholly so,
  Since quickened by thy breath;
O lead me, wheresoe'er I go,
  Through this day's life or death! 44

This day be bread and peace my lot:
  All else beneath the sun
Thou know'st if best bestowed or not,
  And let thy will be done. 48

To Thee, whose temple is all Space,
  Whose altar, earth, sea, skies,
One chorus let all Being raise,
  All Nature's incense rise! 52

1738. *Alexander Pope.*

THE DYING CHRISTIAN TO HIS SOUL

VITAL spark of heav'nly flame!
Quit, O quit this mortal frame:
Trembling, hoping, ling'ring, flying,
Oh, the pain, the bliss of dying!
Cease, fond Nature, cease thy strife,
And let me languish into life! 6

Hark! they whisper; Angels say,
Sister Spirit, come away!
What is this absorbs me quite?
Steals my senses, shuts my sight,
Drowns my spirits, draws my breath?
Tell me, my Soul, can this be Death? 12

The world recedes; it disappears!
Heav'n opens on my eyes! my ears
With sounds seraphic ring:
Lend, lend your wings! I mount! I fly!
O Grave! where is thy Victory?
O Death! where is thy Sting? 18

1712. *Alexander Pope.*

THE QUIET HEART

QUIET, Lord, my froward heart:
  Make me teachable and mild,
Upright, simple, free from art,—
  Make me as a weanèd child:
From distrust and envy free,
Pleased with all that pleases Thee. 6

What Thou shalt to-day provide,
  Let me as a child receive;
What to-morrow may betide,
  Calmly to Thy wisdom leave;
'T is enough that Thou wilt care:
Why should I the burden bear? 12

As a little child relies
  On a care beyond his own,
Knows he 's neither strong nor wise,
  Fears to stir a step alone;
Let me thus with Thee abide,
As my Father, Guard, and Guide. 18

1779. *John Newton.*

REFUGE

JESU, Lover of my soul,
  Let me to Thy bosom fly,
While the nearer waters roll,
  While the tempest still is high:

Refuge

Hide me, O my Saviour, hide
  Till the storm of life is past,
Safe into the haven guide,
  O receive my soul at last! 8

Other refuge have I none;
  Hangs my helpless soul on Thee:
Leave, ah! leave me not alone,
  Still support and comfort me!
All my trust on Thee is stay'd,
  All my help from Thee I bring:
Cover my defenceless head
  With the shadow of Thy wing! 16

Wilt Thou not regard my call?
  Wilt Thou not accept my prayer?
Lo! I sink, I faint, I fall—
  Lo! on Thee I cast my care!
Reach me out Thy gracious hand:
  While I of Thy strength receive,
Hoping against hope I stand,
  Dying, and behold I live! 24

Plenteous grace with Thee is found,
  Grace to cover all my sin;
Let the healing streams abound;
  Make and keep me pure within:—
Thou of Life the Fountain art,
  Freely let me take of Thee;
Spring Thou up within my heart,—
  Rise to all eternity! 32

1740. *Charles Wesley.*

THE GOLDEN DOOR

THE door of death is made of gold,
That mortal eyes cannot behold:
But, when the mortal eyes are closed,
And cold and pale the limbs reposed,
The Soul awakes, and, wondering, sees
In her mild hand the golden keys.
The grave is Heaven's golden gate,
And rich and poor around it wait:
O Shepherdess of England's fold,
Behold this gate of pearl and gold! 10

To dedicate to England's Queen
The visions that my soul has seen,
And by her kind permission bring
What I have borne on solemn wing
From the vast regions of the grave,
Before her throne my wings I wave,
Bowing before my sovereign's feet.
The Grave produced these blossoms sweet,
In mild repose from earthly strife;
The blossoms of eternal life. 20

1808. *William Blake.*

MORNING

Hues of the rich unfolding morn,
That, ere the glorious sun be born,
By some soft touch invisible
Around his path are taught to swell;— 4

Thou rustling breeze, so fresh and gay,
That dancest forth at opening day,
And brushing by with joyous wing,
Wakenest each little leaf to sing;— 8

Ye fragrant clouds of dewy steam,
By which deep grove and tangled stream
Pay, for soft rains in season given,
Their tribute to the genial heaven;— 12

Why waste your treasures of delight
Upon our thankless, joyless sight,
Who day by day to sin awake,
Seldom of Heaven and you partake? 16

Oh! timely happy, timely wise,
Hearts that with rising morn arise!
Eyes that the beam celestial view,
Which evermore makes all things new! 20

New every morning is the love
Our wakening and uprising prove;
Through sleep and darkness safely brought,
Restored to life, and power, and thought. 24

New mercies, each returning day,
Hover around us while we pray;
New perils past, new sins forgiven,
New thoughts of God, new hopes of
Heaven. 28

If on our daily course our mind
Be set to hallow all we find,
New treasures still, of countless price,
God will provide for sacrifice. 32

Old friends, old scenes, will lovelier be,
As more of Heaven in each we see:
Some softening gleam of love and prayer
Shall dawn on every cross and care. 36

As for some dear familiar strain
Untired we ask, and ask again,
Ever, in its melodious store,
Finding a spell unheard before— 40

Such is the bliss of souls serene,
When they have sworn, and steadfast mean,
Counting the cost, in all t' espy
Their God, in all themselves deny. 44

Oh, could we learn that sacrifice,
What lights would all around us rise!
How would our hearts with wisdom talk
Along Life's dullest, dreariest walk! 48

We need not bid, for cloister'd cell,
Our neighbour and our work farewell,
Nor strive to wind ourselves too high
For sinful man beneath the sky: 52

The trivial round, the common task,
Would furnish all we ought to ask—
Room to deny ourselves; a road
To bring us, daily, nearer God. 56

Seek we no more; content with these,
Let present Rapture, Comfort, Ease,
As Heaven shall bid them, come and go—
The secret this of Rest below. 60

Only, O Lord, in Thy dear love
Fit us for perfect Rest above;
And help us, this and every day,
To live more nearly as we pray. 64

1827. *John Keble.*

EVENING

'T is gone, that bright and orbèd blaze,
Fast fading from our wistful gaze;
Yon mantling cloud has hid from sight
The last faint pulse of quivering light. 4

In darkness and in weariness
The traveller on his way must press;
No gleam to watch on tree or tower,
Whiling away the lonesome hour. 8

Sun of my soul! Thou Saviour dear,
It is not night if Thou be near:
Oh! may no earth-born cloud arise
To hide Thee from Thy servant's eyes. 12

When round thy wondrous works below
My searching rapturous glance I throw,
Tracing out Wisdom, Power, and Love,
In earth or sky, in stream or grove— 16

Or by the light Thy words disclose
Watch Time's full river as it flows,
Scanning Thy gracious Providence,
Where not too deep for mortal sense; 20

When with dear friends sweet talk I hold,
And all the flowers of life unfold—
Let not my heart within me burn,
Except in all I Thee discern. 24

When the soft dews of kindly sleep
My wearied eyelids gently steep,
Be my last thought, how sweet to rest
For ever on my Saviour's breast. 28

Abide with me from morn till eve,
For without Thee I cannot live:

Evening

Abide with me when night is nigh,
For without thee I dare not die. 32

Thou Framer of light and dark,
Steer through the tempest Thine own ark:
Amid the howling wintry sea
We are in port if we have Thee. 36

The Rulers of this Christian land,
'Twixt Thee and us ordained to stand,—
Guide Thou their course, O Lord, aright,
Let all do all as in Thy sight. 40

Oh! by Thine own sad burthen, borne
So meekly up the hill of scorn,
Teach Thou Thy Priests their daily cross
To bear as Thine, nor count it loss! 44

If some poor wandering child of Thine
Have spurn'd, to-day, the voice divine,
Now, Lord, the gracious work begin;
Let him no more lie down in sin. 48

Watch by the sick: enrich the poor
With blessings from Thy boundless store:
Be every mourner's sleep to-night
Like infants' slumbers, pure and light. 52

Come near and bless us when we wake,
Ere through the world our way we take,
Till in the ocean of Thy love
We lose ourselves in Heaven above. 56

1827. *John Keble.*

A CHRISTMAS HYMN

It was the calm and silent night!
  Seven hundred years and fifty-three
Had Rome been growing up to might,
  And now was Queen of land and sea.
No sound was heard of clashing wars;
  Peace brooded o'er the hush'd domain;
Apollo, Pallas, Jove and Mars,
  Held undisturb'd their ancient reign,
    In the solemn midnight
      Centuries ago! 10

'T was in the calm and silent night!
  The senator of haughty Rome
Impatient urged his chariot's flight,
  From lordly revel rolling home.
Triumphal arches gleaming swell
  His breast with thoughts of boundless sway;
What reck'd the Roman what befell
  A paltry province far away,
    In the solemn midnight
      Centuries ago! 20

Within that province far away
  Went plodding home a weary boor:
A streak of light before him lay,
  Fall'n through a half-shut stable door

Across his path. He pass'd—for nought
  Told what was going on within;
How keen the stars! his only thought;
  The air how calm and cold and thin,
    In the solemn midnight
      Centuries ago! 30

O strange indifference!—low and high
  Drows'd over common joys and cares:
The earth was still—but knew not why;
  The world was listening—unawares.
How calm a moment may precede
  One that shall thrill the world for ever!
To that still moment none would heed,
  Man's doom was link'd, no more to sever,
    In the solemn midnight
      Centuries ago! 40

It *is* the calm and silent night!
  A thousand bells ring out, and throw
Their joyous peals abroad, and smite
  The darkness, charm'd and holy *now.*
The night that erst no name had worn,
  To it a happy name is given;
For in that stable lay new-born
  The peaceful Prince of Earth and Heaven,
    In the solemn midnight
      Centuries ago! 50

1837. *Alfred Domett.*

ABIDE WITH ME

Abide with me! Fast falls the eventide;
The darkness deepens: Lord, with me abide!
When other helpers fail, and comforts flee,
Help of the helpless, O abide with me! 4

Swift to its close ebbs out life's little day;
Earth's joys grow dim; its glories pass away:
Change and decay in all around I see;
O Thou, who changest not, abide with me! 8

Not a brief glance I beg, a passing word,
But as Thou dwell'st with Thy disciples, Lord,
Familiar, condescending, patient, free,
Come, not to sojourn, but abide, with me! 12

Come not in terrors, as the King of kings;
But kind and good, with healing in Thy wings:
Tears for all woes, a heart for every plea:—
Come, Friend of sinners, and thus bide with
me! 16

Thou on my head in early youth didst smile,
And, though rebellious and perverse meanwhile,
Thou hast not left me, oft as I left Thee.
On to the close, O Lord, abide with me! 20

I need Thy presence every passing hour:
What but Thy grace can foil the Tempter's
power?
Who like Thyself my guide and stay can be?
Through cloud and sunshine, O abide with me! 24

I fear no foe with Thee at hand to bless:
Ills have no weight, and tears no bitterness.
Where is Death's sting? where, Grave, thy
victory?
—I triumph still, if Thou abide with me. 28

Hold Thou Thy Cross before my closing eyes;
Shine through the gloom, and point me to the
skies:
Heaven's morning breaks, and earth's vain
shadows flee:—
In life and death, O Lord, abide with me! 32

1850. *Henry Francis Lyte.*

THE WILL OF GOD

I WORSHIP Thee, sweet Will of God!
And all Thy ways adore,
And every day I live, I seem
To love Thee more and more. 4

Thou wert the end, the blessèd rule
Of our Saviour's toils and tears;
Thou wert the passion of His Heart
Those Three-and-thirty years. 8

And He hath breathed into my soul
  A special love of Thee,
A love to lose my will in His,
  And by that loss be free. 12

He always wins who sides with God,
  To him no chance is lost;
God's Will is sweetest to him, when
  It triumphs at his cost. 16

When obstacles and trials seem
  Like prison-walls to be,
I do the little I can do,
  And leave the rest to Thee. 20

1849. *Frederick William Faber*

GOD'S WAY

Thy way, not mine, O Lord,
  However dark it be!
Lead me by Thine own hand,
  Choose out the path for me. 4

Smooth let it be or rough,
  It will be still the best;
Winding or straight, it leads
  Right onward to Thy rest. 8

I dare not choose my lot;
  I would not, if I might;
Choose Thou for me, my God;
  So shall I walk aright. 12

The kingdom that I seek
  Is Thine; so let the way
That leads to it be Thine;
  Else I must surely stray. 16

Take Thou my cup, and it
  With joy or sorrow fill,
As best to Thee may seem;
  Choose Thou my good and ill; 20

Choose Thou for me my friends,
  My sickness or my health;
Choose Thou my cares for me,
  My poverty or wealth. 24

Not mine, not mine the choice,
  In things or great or small;
Be Thou my guide, my strength,
  My wisdom, and my all! 28

1857. *Horatius Bonar.*

SENSITIVENESS

TIME was, I shrank from what was right
  From fear of what was wrong;
I would not brave the sacred fight,
  Because the foe was strong. 4

But now I cast that finer sense
  And sorer shame aside;

Such dread of sin was indolence,
  Such aim at Heaven was pride. 8

So, when my Saviour calls, I rise
  And calmly do my best;
Leaving to Him, with silent eyes
  Of hope and fear, the rest. 12

I step, I mount where He has led;
  Men count my haltings o'er;—
I know them; yet, though self I dread,
  I love His precept more. 16

1833. 1836. *John Henry Newman.*

FLOWERS WITHOUT FRUIT

Prune thou thy words, the thoughts control
  That o'er thee swell and throng;
They will condense within thy soul,
  And change to purpose strong. 4

But he who lets his feelings run
  In soft luxurious flow,
Shrinks when hard service must be done,
  And faints at every woe. 8

Faith's meanest deed more favour bears,
  Where hearts and wills are weigh'd,
Than brightest transports, choicest prayers,
  Which bloom their hour and fade. 12

1833. *John Henry Newman.*

"O MAY I JOIN THE CHOIR INVISIBLE!"

O MAY I join the choir invisible
Of those immortal dead who live again
In minds made better by their presence: live
In pulses stirred to generosity,
In deeds of daring rectitude, in scorn
Of miserable aims that end with self,
In thoughts sublime that pierce the night like
    stars,
And with their mild persistence urge man's
    search
To vaster issues.
                So to live is heaven: 10
To make undying music in the world,
Breathing as beauteous order that controls
With growing sway the growing life of man.
So we inherit that sweet purity
For which we struggled, failed, and agonized
With widening retrospect that bred despair.
Rebellious flesh that would not be subdued,
A vicious parent shaming still its child
Poor anxious penitence, is quick dissolved;
Its discords, quenched by meeting harmonies, 20
Die in the large and charitable air.

And all our rarer, better, truer self,
That sobbed religiously in yearning song,
That watched to ease the burthen of the world,
Laboriously tracing what must be,
And what may yet be better—saw within
A worthier image for the sanctuary,
And shaped it forth before the multitude
Divinely human, raising worship so
To higher reverence more mixed with love— 30
That better self shall live till human Time
Shall fold its eyelids, and the human sky
Be gathered like a scroll within the tomb,
Unread forever.
This is life to come,
Which martyred men have made more glorious
For us who strive to follow. May I reach
That purest heaven, be to other souls
The cup of strength in some great agony,
Enkindle generous ardor, feed pure love, 40
Beget the smiles that have no cruelty—
Be the sweet presence of a good diffused,
And in diffusion ever more intense.
So shall I join the choir invisible
Whose music is the gladness of the world.

1867. 1874. *Marian Evans Cross.*

A LIFE HID WITH CHRIST

I HAVE a life with Christ to live,
But, ere I live it, must I wait
Till learning can clear answer give
Of this and that book's date?

I have a life in Christ to live,
  I have a death in Christ to die;—
And must I wait, till science give
  All doubts a full reply? 3

Nay rather, while the sea of doubt
Is raging wildly round about,
Questioning of life and death and sin,
Let me but creep within
Thy fold, O Christ, and at Thy feet
Take but the lowest seat,
And hear Thine awful voice repeat
In gentlest accents, heavenly sweet,
  Come unto Me, and rest:
  Believe Me, and be blest. 18

John Campbell Shairp.

CONSTANCY

'Twixt gleams of joy and clouds of doubt
  Our feelings come and go;
Our best estate is toss'd about
  In ceaseless ebb and flow. 4

No mood of feeling, form of thought,
  Is constant for a day;
But Thou, O Lord! Thou changest not;
  The same Thou art alway. 8

I grasp Thy strength, make it mine own,
  My heart with peace is blest;

I lose my hold, and then comes down
  Darkness and cold unrest. 12

Let me no more my comfort draw
  From my frail hold of Thee,—
In this alone rejoice with awe;
  Thy mighty grasp of me. 16

Out of that weak unquiet drift
  That comes but to depart,
To that pure Heaven my spirit lift
  Where Thou unchanging art. 20

Lay hold of me with Thy strong grasp,
  Let Thy Almighty arm
In its embrace my weakness clasp,
  And I shall fear no harm. 24

Thy purpose of eternal good
  Let me but surely know;
On this I 'll lean, let changing mood
  And feeling come or go; 28

Glad when Thy sunshine fills my soul;
  Not lorn when clouds o'ercast;
Since Thou within Thy sure control
  Of Love dost hold me fast. 32

1864? *John Campbell Shairp.*

MY PSALM

I MOURN no more my vanished years:
  Beneath a tender rain,
And April rain of smiles and tears,
  My heart is young again. 4

The west-winds blow, and, singing low,
  I hear the glad streams run;
The windows of my soul I throw
  Wide open to the sun. 8

No longer forward nor behind
  I look in hope or fear;
But, grateful, take the good I find,
  The best of now and here. 12

I plough no more a desert land,
  To harvest weed and tare;
The manna dropping from God's hand
  Rebukes my painful care. 16

I break my pilgrim staff,—I lay
  Aside the toiling oar;
The angel sought so far away
  I welcome at my door. 20

The airs of spring may never play
  Among the ripening corn,
Nor freshness of the flowers of May
  Blow through the autumn morn; 24

Yet shall the blue-eyed gentian look
  Through fringèd lids to heaven,
And the pale aster in the brook
  Shall see its image given;— 28

The woods shall wear their robes of praise,
  The south-wind softly sigh,
And sweet, calm days in golden haze
  Melt down the amber sky. 32

Not less shall manly deed and word
  Rebuke an age of wrong;
The graven flowers that wreathe the sword
  Make not the blade less strong. 36

But smiting hands shall learn to heal,—
  To build as to destroy;
Nor less my heart for others feel
  That I the more enjoy. 40

All as God wills, who wisely heeds
  To give or to withhold,
And knoweth more of all my needs
  Than all my prayers have told! 44

Enough that blessings undeserved
  Have marked my erring track;—

That wheresoe'er my feet have swerved,
His chastening turned me back;— 48

That more and more a Providence
Of love is understood,
Making the springs of time and sense
Sweet with eternal good;— 52

That death seems but a covered way
Which opens into light,
Wherein no blinded child can stray
Beyond the Father's sight;— 56

That care and trial seem at last,
Through Memory's sunset air,
Like mountain-ranges overpast,
In purple distance fair;— 60

That all the jarring notes of life
Seem blending in a psalm,
And all the angles of its strife
Slow rounding into calm. 64

And so the shadows fall apart,
And so the west-winds play;
And all the windows of my heart
I open to the day. 68

1859. *John Greenleaf Whittier.*

PARADAISI GLORIA

THERE is a city, builded by no hand,
  And unapproachable by sea or shore,
And unassailable by any band
  Of storming soldiery for evermore. 4

There we no longer shall divide our time
  By acts or pleasures,—doing petty things
Of work or warfare, merchandise or rhyme;
  But we shall sit beside the silver springs 8

That flow from God's own footstool, and behold
  Sages and martyrs, and those blessed few
Who loved us once and were beloved of old
  To dwell with them and walk with them
    anew, 12

In alterations of sublime repose,
  Musical motion, the perpetual play
Of every faculty that Heaven bestows
  Through the bright, busy, and eternal day. 16

1872. *Thomas William Parsons.*

THE ETERNAL GOODNESS

O FRIENDS! with whom my feet have trod
  The quiet aisles of prayer,
Glad witness to your zeal for God
  And love of man I bear. 4

The Eternal Goodness

I trace your lines of argument;
  Your logic linked and strong
I weigh as one who dreads dissent,
  And fears a doubt as wrong. 8

But still my human hands are weak
  To hold your iron creeds:
Against the words ye bid me speak
  My heart within me pleads. 12

Who fathoms the Eternal Thought?
  Who talks of scheme and plan?
The Lord is God! He needeth not
  The poor device of man. 16

I walk with bare, hushed feet the ground
  Ye tread with boldness shod;
I dare not fix with mete and bound
  The love and power of God. 20

Ye praise His justice; even such
  His pitying love I deem:
Ye seek a king; I fain would touch
  The robe that hath no seam. 24

Ye see the curse which overbroods
  A world of pain and loss;
I hear our Lord's beatitudes
  And prayer upon the cross. 28

More than our schoolmen teach, within
  Myself, alas! I know

Too dark ye cannot paint the sin,
  Too small the merit show. 32

I bow my forehead to the dust,
  I veil mine eyes for shame,
And urge, in trembling self-distrust,
  A prayer without a claim. 36

I see the wrong that round me lies,
  I feel the guilt within;
I hear, with groan and travail-cries,
  The world confess its sin. 40

Yet, in the maddening maze of things,
  And tossed by storm and flood,
To one fixed trust my spirit clings;
  I know that God is good! 44

Not mine to look where cherubim
  And seraphs may not see,
But nothing can be good in Him
  Which evil is in me. 48

The wrong that pains my soul below
  I dare not throne above,
I know not of His hate,—I know
  His goodness and His love. 52

I dimly guess from blessings known
  Of greater out of sight,
And, with the chastened Psalmist, own
  His judgments too are right. 56

I long for household voices gone,
For vanished smiles I long,
But God hath led my dear ones on,
And He can do no wrong. 60

I know not what the future hath
Of marvel or surprise,
Assured alone that life and death
His mercy underlies. 64

And if my heart and flesh are weak
To bear an untried pain,
The bruised reed He will not break,
But strengthen and sustain. 68

No offering of my own I have,
Nor works my faith to prove;
I can but give the gifts he gave,
And plead His love for love. 72

And so beside the Silent Sea
I wait the muffled oar;
No harm from Him can come to me
On ocean or on shore. 76

I know not where His islands lift
Their fronded palms in air;
I only know I cannot drift
Beyond His love and care. 80

O brothers! if my faith is vain,
If hopes like these betray,

Pray for me that my feet may gain
  The sure and safer way. 84

And Thou, O Lord! by whom are seen
  Thy creatures as they be,
Forgive me if too close I lean
  My human heart on Thee! 88

1865. *John Greenleaf Whittier.*

SELECTIONS
FROM THE LATER POETRY

Elegies and Hymns

Elegies and Poems on Death
Hymns and Poems of Faith

Poems of the Great War

BIRTHRIGHT*

LORD Rameses of Egypt sighed
  Because a summer evening passed;
And little Ariadne cried
  That summer fancy fell at last
To dust; and young Verona died
  When beauty's hour was overcast. 6

Theirs was the bitterness we know
  Because the clouds of hawthorn keep
So short a state, and kisses go
  To tombs unfathomably deep,
While Rameses and Romeo
  And little Ariadne sleep. 12

John Drinkwater.

ATROPOS

ATROPOS, dread
  One of the Three,
Holding the thread
  Woven for me; 4

Grimly thy shears,
  Steely and bright,

---

* Used by permission of the author and of the publisher Houghton Mifflin Company.

Menace the years
 Left for delight. 8

Grant it may chance,
 Just as they close,
June may entrance
 Earth with the rose; 12

Reigning as though,
 Bliss to the breath,
Endless and no
 Whisper of death. 16

John Myers O'Hara.

ENVOI*

OH SEEK me not within a tomb—
 Thou shalt not find me in the clay!
I pierce a little wall of gloom
 To mingle with the day! 4

I brothered with the things that pass,
 Poor giddy joy and puckered grief;
I go to brother with the grass
 And with the sunning leaf. 8

Not death can sheathe me in a shroud;
 A joy-sword whetted keen with pain,

*Reprinted, with the author's permission, from "The Quest," published by The Macmillan Company.

I join the armies of the cloud,
The lightning and the rain. 12

Oh, subtle in the sap athrill,
Athletic in the glad uplift,
A portion of the cosmic will,
I pierce the planet-drift. 16

My God and I shall interknit
As rain and ocean, breath and air;
And oh, the luring thought of it
Is prayer! 20

John G. Neihardt.

THE OXEN

CHRISTMAS EVE, and twelve of the clock.
"Now they are all on their knees,"
An elder said as we sat in a flock
By the embers in hearthside ease. 4

We pictured the meek mild creatures where
They dwelt in their strawy pen,
Nor did it occur to one of us there
To doubt they were kneeling then. 8

So fair a fancy few believe
In these years! Yet, I feel,
If someone said on Christmas Eve
"Come; see the oxen kneel 12

"In the lonely barton by yonder coomb
  Our childhood used to know,"
I should go with him in the gloom,
  Hoping it might be so. 16

Thomas Hardy.

TRYSTE NOËL

THE Ox he openeth wide the Doore,
And from the Snowe he calls her inne,
And he hath seen her Smile therefor,
Our Ladye without Sinne.
Now soon from Sleep 5
A Starre shall leap,
And soone arrive both King and Hinde:
  Amen, Amen:
But O, the Place co'd I but finde!

The Ox hath hush'd his voyce and bent 10
Trewe eyes of Pitty ore the Mow,
And on his lovelie Neck, forspent,
The Blessèd layes her Browe.
Around her feet
Full Warme and Sweete 15
His bowerie Breath doth meeklie dwell:
  Amen, Amen:
But sore am I with Vaine Travèl!

The Ox is host in Judah stall
And Host of more than onelie one, 20
For close she gathereth withal

Our Lorde her littel Sonne.
Glad Hinde and King
Their Gyfte may bring,
But wo'd to-night my Teares were there, 25
Amen, Amen:
Between her Bosom and His hayre!

Louise Imogen Guiney.

IN THE HOSPITAL

BECAUSE on the branch that is tapping my pane
A sun-wakened leaf-bud, uncurled,
Is bursting its rusty brown sheathing in twain,
I know there is Spring in the world. 4

Because through the sky-patch whose azure and white
My window frames all the day long,
A yellow-bird dips for an instant of flight,
I know there is Song. 8

Because even here in this Mansion of Woe
Where creep the dull hours, leaden-shod,
Compassion and Tenderness aid me, I know 12
There is God.

Arthur Guiterman.

CREATION

IN THE beginning, there was nought
But heaven, one Majesty of Light,
Beyond all speech, beyond all thought,
Beyond all depth, beyond all height,
Consummate heaven, the first and last,
Enfolding in its perfect prime
No future rushing to the past,
But one rapt Now, that knew not Space or Time. 8

Formless it was, being gold on gold,
And void—but with that complete Life
Where music could no wings unfold
Till lo, God smote the strings of strife!
"Myself unto Myself am Throne,
Myself unto Myself am Thrall
I that am All am all alone,"
He said, "Yea, I have nothing, having all." 16

And, gathering round His mount of bliss
The angel-squadrons of His will,
He said, "One battle yet there is
To win, one vision to fulfil!
Since heaven where'er I gaze expands,
And power that knows no strife or cry,
Weakness shall bind and pierce My hands
And make a world for Me wherein to die. 24

All might, all vastness and all glory
Being Mine, I must descend and make
Out of My heart a song, a story
Of little hearts that burn and break;
Out of My passion without end
I will make little azure seas,
And into small sad fields descend
And make green grass, white daisies, rustling
trees." 32

Then shrank His angels, knowing He thrust
His arms out East and West and gave
For every little dream of dust
Part of His Life as to a grave!
"*Enough, O Father, for Thy words*
Have pierced Thy hands!" But, low and sweet,
He said "Sunsets and streams and birds,
And drifting clouds!"—The purple stained His
feet.— 40

"*Enough!*" His angels moaned in fear,
"*Father, Thy words have pierced Thy side!*"
He whispered, "Roses shall grow there,
And there must be a hawthorn-tide,
And ferns, dewy at dawn," and still
They moaned—"*Enough, the red drops bleed!*"
"And," sweet and low, "on every hill,"
He said, "I will have flocks and lambs to
lead." 48

His angels bowed their heads beneath
Their wings till that great pang was gone:

"Pour not Thy soul out unto Death!"
They moaned, and still His Love flowed on,
"There shall be small white wings to stray
From bliss to bliss, from bloom to bloom,
And blue flowers in the wheat; and——" *"Stay!*
Speak not," they cried, *"the word that seals Thy tomb!"* 56

He spake—"I have thought of a little child
That I will have there to embark
On small adventures in the wild,
And front slight perils in the dark;
And I will hide from him and lure
His laughing eyes with suns and moons,
And rainbows that shall not endure;
And—when he is weary sing him drowsy tunes." 64

His angels fell before Him weeping
"Enough! Tempt not the Gates of Hell!"
He said "His soul is in his keeping
That we may love each other well,
And lest the dark too much affright him;
I will strow countless little stars
Across his childish skies to light him
That he may wage in peace his mimic wars; 72

And oft forget Me as he plays
With swords and childish merchandise;
Or with his elfin balance weighs,
Or with his foot-rule metes, the skies;
Or builds his castles by the deep,

Or tunnels through the rocks, and then—
Turn to Me as he falls asleep,
And, in his dreams, feel for My hand again. 80

And when he is older he shall be
My friend and walk here at My side;
Or—when he wills—grow young with Me,
And, to that happy world where once we died
Descending through the calm blue weather,
Buy life once more with our immortal breath,
And wander through the little fields together,
And taste of Love and Death." 88

Alfred Noyes.

POEMS OF THE GREAT WAR

FALL IN!

WE THOUGHT that reason had mastered men,
  That peace of the world was lord,
That never the roll of the drum again
  Should quicken the thirsty sword— 4
But our bubble broke with a sudden blow,
  And we heard like the trumpet's din
That levelled the walls of Jericho—
  The old stern cry—"*Fall in!*" 8

We were numb, amazed, we were sick and dazed
  With a horror past belief.
Silent we stood while Belgium blazed
  In her martyr's glory of grief. 12
Then it came so near that we needs must hear,
  For the cry of our murdered kin
Drove in our heart like a searching spear
  The call of the hour—"*Fall in!*" 16

Not in the flush of a barren thrill
  Do we come to our deed at last.
We have weighed our will, we must do our will,
  For the doubting-time is past. 20
We have faced our souls in the sleepless night,
  And what shall we fear but sin?
Not for love of the fight, but for love of the right,
  In the name of our God—"*Fall in!*" 24

Amelia Josephine Burr.

SOLDIER, SOLDIER

SOLDIER, soldier, off to the war,
Take me a letter to my sweetheart O.
He's gone away to France
With his carbine and his lance,
And a lock of brown hair of his sweetheart O. 5

Fair maid of London, happy may you be
To know so much of your sweetheart O.
There's not a handsome lad,
To get the chance he's had,
But would skip, with a kiss for his sweetheart O. 10

Soldier, soldier, whatever shall I do
If the cruel Germans take my sweetheart O?
They'll pen him in the jail
And starve him thin and pale,
With never a kind word from his sweetheart O. 15

Fair maid of London, is that all you see
Of the lad you've taken for your sweetheart O?
He'll make his prison ring
With his God Save the King
And his God bless the blue eyes of my sweetheart O! 20

Soldier, soldier, if by shot or shell
They wound him, my dear lad, my sweetheart O,
He'll lie bleeding in the rain
And call me, all in vain,
Crying for the fingers of his sweetheart O. 25

Pretty one, pretty one, now take a word from me:
Don't you grudge the life-blood of your sweet-
heart O.
For you must understand
He gives it to our land.
And proud should fly the colors of his sweet-
heart O. 30

Soldier, soldier, my heart is growing cold—
If a German shot kill my sweetheart O!
I could not lift my head
If my dear love lay dead
With his wide eyes waiting for his sweetheart O. 35

Poor child, poor child, go to church and pray,
Pray God to spare you your sweetheart O.
But if he live or die
The English flag must fly,
And England take care of his sweetheart O! 40

Maurice Hewlett.

THE YOUNG DEAD

Ah, how I pity the young dead who gave
All that they were, and might become, that we
With tired eyes should watch this perfect sea

Re-weave its patterning of silver wave
Round scented cliffs of arbutus and bay. 5

No more shall any rose along the way,
The myrtled way that wanders to the shore,
Nor jonquil-twinkling meadows any more,
Nor the warm lavender that takes the spray,
Smell only of sea-salt and the sun. 10

But, through recurring seasons, every one
Shall speak to us with lips the darkness closes,
Shall look at us with eyes that missed the roses,
Clutch us with hands whose work was just begun,
Laid idle now beneath the earth we tread— 15

And always we shall walk with the young dead—
Ah, how I pity the young dead, whose eyes
Strain through the sod to see the perfect skies,
Who feel the new wheat springing in their stead,
And the lark singing for them overhead! 20

Edith Wharton.

IN FLANDERS FIELDS*

IN FLANDERS fields the poppies blow
Between the crosses, row on row,
That mark our place, and in the sky,
The larks, still bravely singing, fly,
Scarce heard amid the guns below. 5

We are the dead; short days ago
We lived, felt dawn, saw sunset glow,

*From "In Flanders Fields", courtesy of G. P. Putnam's Sons, Publishers, New York and London.

Loved and were loved, and now we lie
In Flanders fields. 10

Take up our quarrel with the foe!
To you from failing hands we throw
The torch; be yours to hold it high!
If ye break faith with us who die,
We shall not sleep, though poppies grow 15
In Flanders fields.

John McCrae.

I HAVE A RENDEZVOUS WITH DEATH*

I HAVE a rendezvous with Death
At some disputed barricade,
When Spring comes back with rustling shade
And apple-blossoms fill the air—
I have a rendezvous with Death 5
When Spring brings back blue days and fair.
It may be he shall take my hand
And lead me into his dark land
And close my eyes and quench my breath—
It may be I shall pass him still. 10
I have a rendezvous with Death
On some scarred slope of battered hill
When Spring comes round again this year
And the first meadow-flowers appear.

*Used by permission of Charles Scribner's Sons, by whom this poem is copyrighted.

God knows 't were better to be deep 15
Pillowed in silk and scented down,
Where Love throbs out in blissful sleep,
Pulse nigh to pulse, and breath to breath,
Where hushed awakenings are dear . . .
But I've a rendezvous with Death 20
At midnight in some flaming town,
When Spring trips north again this year,
And I to my pledged word am true,
I shall not fail that rendezvous.

Alan Seeger.

THE FEAR*

I DO not fear to die
'Neath the open sky,
To meet death in the fight
Face to face, upright. 4

But when at last we creep
Into a hole to sleep,
I tremble, cold with dread,
Lest I wake up dead. 8

Wilfrid Wilson Gibson.

BACK*

THEY ask me where I've been,
And what I've done and seen.
But what can I reply
Who know it wasn't I,

*Used by permission of the publishers, The Macmillan Co.

But some one just like me, 5
Who went across the sea
And with my head and hands
Killed men in foreign lands . . .
Though I must bear the blame
Because he bore my name. 10

Wilfrid Wilson Gibson.

THE RETURN*

HE WENT, and he was gay to go:
And I smiled on him as he went.
My son—'twas well he couldn't know
My darkest dread, nor what it meant— 4

Just what it meant to smile and smile
And let my son go cheerily—
My son . . . and wondering all the while
What stranger would come back to me. 8

Wilfrid Wilson Gibson.

INTO BATTLE

THE naked earth is warm with spring,
  And with green grass and bursting trees
Leans to the sun's gaze glorying,
  And quivers in the sunny breeze;

*Used by permission of the publishers, The Macmillan Co.

And life is colour and warmth and light, 5
  And a striving evermore for these;
And he is dead who will not fight;
  And who dies fighting has increase.

The fighting man shall from the sun
  Take warmth, and life from the glowing
    earth; 10
Speed with the light-foot winds to run
  And with the trees to newer birth;
And find, when fighting shall be done,
  Great rest, and fullness after dearth.

All the bright company of Heaven 15
  Hold him in their high comradeship,
The Dog-Star, and the Sisters Seven,
  Orion's Belt and sworded hip.
The woodland trees that stand together,
  They stand to him each one a friend; 20
They gently speak in the windy weather;
  They guide to valley and ridge's end.
The kestrel hovering by day,
  And the little owls that call by night,
Bid him be swift and keen as they, 25
As keen of ear, as swift of sight.

The blackbird sings to him, "Brother, brother,
  If this be the last song you shall sing,
Sing well, for you may not sing another;
  Brother, sing." 30

In dreary, doubtful, waiting hours,
  Before the brazen frenzy starts,

The horses show him nobler powers
O patient eyes, courageous hearts!

And when the burning moment breaks, 35
And all things else are out of mind,
And only joy of battle takes
Him by the throat, and makes him blind,

Through joy and blindness he shall know
Not caring much to know, that still 40
Nor lead nor steel shall reach him, so
That it be not the Destined Will.

The thundering line of battle stands,
And in the air death moans and sings;
But Day shall clasp him with strong hands, 45
And Night shall fold him in soft wings.

Julian Grenfell

IT'S A QUEER TIME*

It's hard to know if you're alive or dead
When steel and fire go roaring through your head.

One moment you'll be crouching at your gun
Traversing, mowing heaps down half in fun:
The next, you choke and clutch at your right breast— 5
No time to think—leave all—and off you go. . . .

*Used by arrangement with the author's agents, James B. Pinker and Son, London.

To Treasure Island where the spice winds
    blow,
To lovely groves of mango, quince and lime?
Breathe no good-bye, but ho, for the Red West!
    It's a queer time. 10

You're charging madly at them yelling "Fag!"
When somehow something gives and your feet
    drag.
You fall and strike your head; yet feel no pain
And find . . . you're digging tunnels through
    the hay
In the Big Barn, 'cause it's a rainy day. 15
Oh springy hay, and lovely beams to climb!
You're back in the old sailor suit again.
    It's a queer time.

Or you'll be dozing safe in your dug-out—
A great roar—the trench shakes and falls
    about— 20
You're struggling, gasping, struggling, then. . .
    hullo!
Elsie comes tripping gaily down the trench,
Hanky to nose—that lyddite makes a stench—
Getting her pinafore all over grime.
Funny! because she died ten years ago! 25
  It's a queer time.

The trouble is, things happen much too quick;
Up jump the Boches, rifles thump and click,
You stagger, and the whole scene fades away:
Even good Christians don't like passing
    straight 30

From Tipperary or their Hymn of Hate
To Alleluiah-chanting, and the chime
Of golden harps . . . and . . . I'm not well to-day . . .
It's a queer time.

Robert Graves.

SONGS FROM AN EVIL WOOD

III

THE great guns of England, they listen mile on mile
To the boasts of a broken War-Lord; they lift their throats and smile;
But the old woods are fallen
For a while. 4

The old woods are fallen; yet will they come again;
They will come back some springtime with the warm winds and the rain,
For Nature guardeth her children
Never in vain. 8

They will come back some season; it may be a hundred years;
It is all one to Nature with the centuries that are hers;
She shall bring back her children
And dry all their tears. 12

But the tears of a would-be War-Lord shall never
cease to flow,
He shall weep for the poisoned armies whenever the
gas-winds blow,
He shall always weep for his widows,
And all Hell shall know. 16

The tears of a pitiless Kaiser shallow they'll flow
and wide,
Wide as the desolation made by his silly pride
When he slaughtered a little people
To stab France in her side. 20

Over the ragged cinders they shall flow on and
on
With the listless falling of streams that find not
oblivion,
For ages and ages of years
Till the last star is gone. 24

IV

I met with Death in his country,
With his scythe and his hollow eye,
Walking the roads of Belgium.
I looked and he passed me by. 4

Since he passed me by in Plug Street,
In the wood of the evil name,
I shall not now lie with the heroes,
I shall not share their fame, 8

Dreamers

I shall never be as they are,
  A name in the lands of the Free,
Since I looked on Death in Flanders
  And he did not look at me. 12

Lord Dunsany.

DREAMERS*

SOLDIERS are citizens of death's grey land,
  Drawing no dividend from time's to-morrows.
In the great hour of destiny they stand,
  Each with his feuds, and jealousies, and sorrows.
Soldiers are sworn to action; they must win
  Some flaming, fatal climax with their lives.
Soldiers are dreamers; when the guns begin 7
  They think of firelit homes, clean beds, and wives.

I see them in foul dug-outs, gnawed by rats,
  And in the ruined trenches, lashed with rain,
Dreaming of things they did with balls and bats,
  And mocked by hopeless longing to regain
Bank-holidays, and picture-shows, and spats,
  And going to the office in the train. 14

Siegfried Sassoon.

---

*Reprinted by permission from "Dreamers," by Mr. Siegfried Sassoon, copyright by E. P. Dutton and Company.

EARTH'S EASTER*

(1915)

EARTH has gone up from its Gethsemane,
And now on Golgotha is crucified;
The spear is twisted in the tortured side;
The thorny crown still works its cruelty.
Hark! while the victim suffers on the tree,
There sound through starry spaces, far and wide,
Such words as in the last despair are cried:
"My God! my God! Thou hast forsaken me!"

But when earth's members from the cross are drawn,
And all we love into the grave is gone,
This hope shall be a spark within the gloom:
That, in the glow of some stupendous dawn,
We may go forth to find, where lilies bloom,
Two angels bright before an empty tomb.

Robert Haven Schauffler.

THE NAME OF FRANCE

GIVE us a name to fill the mind
With the shining thoughts that lead mankind,
The glory of learning, the joy of art,—
A name that tells of a splendid part

*Used by permission of the author and of the publisher, Houghton Mifflin Company.

The Name of France

In the long, long toil and the strenuous
fight 5
Of the human race to win its way
From the feudal darkness into the day
Of Freedom, Brotherhood, Equal Right,—
A name like a star, a name of light.
I give you *France*! 10

Give us a name to stir the blood
With a warmer glow and a swifter flood
At the touch of a courage that conquers fear,—
A name like the sound of a trumpet, clear,
And silver-sweet, and iron-strong, 15
That calls three million men to their feet,
Ready to march, and steady to meet
The foes who threaten that name with wrong,—
A name that rings like a battle-song.
I give you *France*! 20

Give us a name to move the heart
With the strength that noble griefs impart,
A name that speaks of the blood outpoured
To save mankind from the sway of the sword,—
A name that calls on the world to share 25
In the burden of sacrificial strife
Where the cause at stake is the world's free life
And the rule of the people everywhere,—
A name like a vow, a name like a prayer.
I give you *France*! 30

Henry van Dyke.

PLACE DE LA CONCORDE

August 14, 1914.

(Since the bombardment of Strasbourg, August 14, 1870, her statue in Paris, representing Alsace, had been draped in mourning by the French people.)

NEAR where the royal victims fell
In days gone by, caught in the swell
Of a ruthless tide
Of human passion, deep and wide:
There where we two 5
A Nation's later sorrow knew—
To-day, O friend! I stood
Amid a self-ruled multitude
That by nor sound nor word
Betrayed how mightily its heart was stirred. 10

A memory Time never could efface—
A memory of Grief—
Like a great Silence brooded o'er the place;
And men breathed hard, as seeking for relief
From an emotion strong 15
That would not cry, though held in check too long.

One felt that joy drew near—
A joy intense that seemed itself to fear—
Brightening in eyes that had been dull,
As all with feeling gazed 20

Place de la Concorde

Upon the Strasbourg figure, raised
Above us—mourning, beautiful!

Then one stood at the statue's base, and spoke—
Men needed not to ask what word;
Each in his breast the message heard, 25
Writ for him by Despair,
That evermore in moving phrase
Breathes from the Invalides and Père Lachaise—
Vainly it seemed, alas!
But now, France looking on the image there, 30
Hope gave her back the lost Alsace.

A deeper hush fell on the crowd:
A sound—the lightest—seemed too loud
(Would, friend, you had been there!)
As to that form the speaker rose, 35
Took from her, fold on fold,
The mournful crape, gray-worn and old,
Her, proudly, to disclose,
And with the touch of tender care
That fond emotion speaks, 40
'Mid tears that none could quite command,
Placed the Tricolor in her hand,
And kissed her on both cheeks!

Florence Earle Coates.

1914

V

THE SOLDIER

If I should die, think only this of me;
That there's some corner of a foreign field
That is forever England. There shall be
In that rich earth a richer dust concealed;
A dust whom England bore, shaped, made aware,
Gave, once, her flowers to love, her ways to roam;
A body of England's, breathing English air, 7
Washed by the rivers, blest by suns of home.
And think, this heart, all evil shed away.
A pulse in the eternal mind, no less
Gives somewhere back the thoughts by England
given;
Her sights and sounds; dreams happy as her day;
And laughter learnt of friends; and gentleness,
In hearts at peace, under an English heaven. 14

Rupert Brooke.

INDEX TO FIRST LINES
VOLS. X-XV

INDEX TO FIRST LINES

VOLS. X—XV

Index to First Lines

Index to First Lines

Index to First Lines

Index to First Lines

Index to First Lines

Index to First Lines

Index to First Lines

Index to First Lines

Index to First Lines

Index to First Lines

Index to First Lines

Index to First Lines

Index to First Lines

Index to First Lines

Index to First Lines

Index to First Lines

Index to First Lines

Index to First Lines

Index to First Lines

Index to First Lines

Index to First Lines

Index to First Lines

Index to First Lines